Enrichment

MATH & READING

Grades 3 & 4

Dear Young Learner,

Welcome to your new *Enrichment Book*. Inside, you'll find lots of fun things to do. You'll find games, puzzles and stories to write. You'll find riddles, contests, and even a few surprises. And best of all, you'll have the chance to share all the fun with your family or friends.

While you are having fun, you will also be learning some important math and reading skills, skills you will be able to use in school and for the rest of your life.

We know this book will be one of your favorite ways to learn-- and to have fun!

Sincerely,

Your Learning Partners at American Education Publishing

Table of Contents
Math Grade 3

Pages

Math Grade 4

Pages

Fractions and Decimals

Problem Solving

Reading Grade 3

Word Skills

Study Skills

Vocabulary

Reading Grade 4

Vocabulary

Study Skills

Comprehension

Forms of Writing

Enrichment
Math Grade 3

AMERICAN
EDUCATION
PUBLISHING

Target Sum

The number at the top of each sign is the target number. Draw a ring around three pairs of numbers whose sum is the target number.

1.

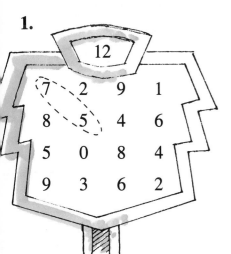

12			
7	2	9	1
8	5	4	6
5	0	8	4
9	3	6	2

2.

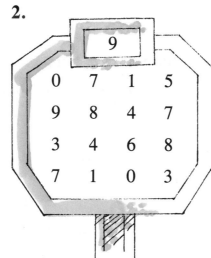

9			
0	7	1	5
9	8	4	7
3	4	6	8
7	1	0	3

3.

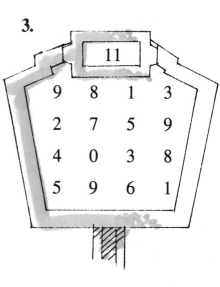

11			
9	8	1	3
2	7	5	9
4	0	3	8
5	9	6	1

4.

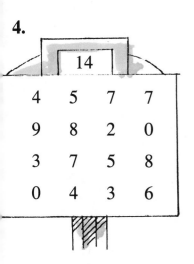

14			
4	5	7	7
9	8	2	0
3	7	5	8
0	4	3	6

5.

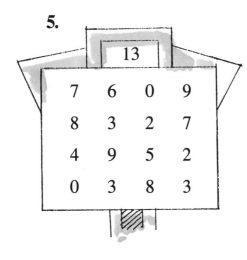

13			
7	6	0	9
8	3	2	7
4	9	5	2
0	3	8	3

6.

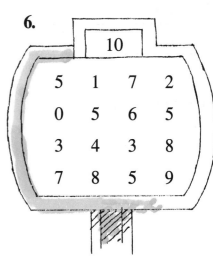

10			
5	1	7	2
0	5	6	5
3	4	3	8
7	8	5	9

Shake-A-Sum

Find an egg carton.

Write the numbers in the sections.

Ask someone to play this game with you.

Play 5 rounds.

In each round:

- Put 2 beans in the carton.
  Close the carton and shake it.

- Open the carton.
  Add the numbers on which the beans land.

- The player with the greatest sum scores a point.

The player with the most points after 5 rounds is the winner.

	Player 1	Player 2
Round 1		
Round 2		
Round 3		
Round 4		
Round 5		

The winner is _____

Adding with Basic Facts

Match It Right

Use these numbers.
Put the correct number in the boxes below.
Cross off the number after you use it.

18   10
11   12
4   9   13
7
3   16
8
6   0   5

1.

17
−9
☐

2.

15
− ☐
9

3.

11
− ☐
7

4.

☐
−9
9

5.

☐
−7
6

6.

14
− ☐
5

7.

☐
−8
8

8.

2
− ☐
2

9.

☐
−2
9

10.

16
− ☐
9

11.

☐
−5
7

12.

☐
− ☐
3

Take 1-2-3

Here is a game for you and a friend.

- Make a pile of 15 chips or coins.
- Decide who plays first.
- Take turns.
- On your turn, take away, 1, 2, or 3 chips.
- The winner is the person who takes the last chip.

Play five games.

Keep track of the winners.

Game	Winner
1	_____
2	_____
3	_____
4	_____
5	_____

Who won more games? _____

Here are some questions for the winner.

1. Did you play first when you won? _____

2. What plan did you use to win? _____

_____

Nines-By-Fingers

You can use your fingers to find the products when multiplying by nine.

Hold out both hands. Think of your fingers numbered 1 through 10.

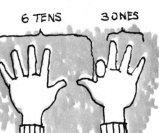

To find 7×9:
Put down finger number 7.
The number of fingers to the left is the number of tens.
The number of fingers to the right is the number of ones.

$7 \times 9 = 63$

Use your fingers to find these products.

1.

$5 \times 9 =$

2.

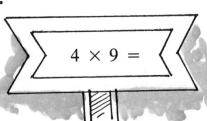

$4 \times 9 =$

3.

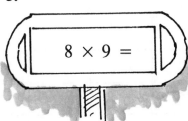

$8 \times 9 =$

4.

$9 \times 9 =$

5.

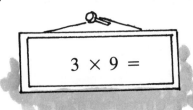

$3 \times 9 =$

6.

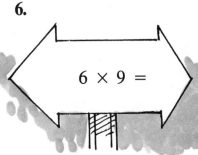

$6 \times 9 =$

Roll-A-Product

Ask someone to play this game with you.

You need 2 number cubes and 2 crayons.

Take turns.

On each turn:

■ Roll 2 number cubes.

■ Multiply the two numbers you roll.

■ Write the product on the playing board if the space is empty.

The first player to write four products in the same row, column, or diagonal is the winner.

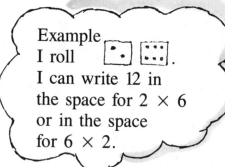

Example
I roll ⚁ ⚅.
I can write 12 in the space for 2 × 6 or in the space for 6 × 2.

Playing Board

×	1	2	3	4	5	6
1						
2						
3						
4						
5						
6						

2 + 6 = 12

6 × 2 = 12

Division Squares

Write the missing numbers.

Make true number sentences across and down.

1.

24	÷	6	=	
÷		÷		÷
8	÷	2	=	
=		=		=
	÷		=	

2.

36	÷	6	=	
÷		÷		÷
9	÷	3	=	
=		=		=
	÷		=	

3.

48	÷	6	=	
÷		÷		÷
8	÷	2	=	
=		=		=
	÷		=	

4.

40	÷	4	=	
÷		÷		÷
8	÷	4	=	
=		=		=
	÷		=	

How Many Please?

Take a look around your kitchen.

Have an adult help you.

1. What can you find that comes 2 in a package?

   _____   _____

2. How many packages would you have to buy if you wanted 8 in all?_____

3. What can you find that comes 4 in a package?

   _____   _____

4. How many packages would you have to buy if you wanted 20 in all?_____

5. What can you find that comes 6 in a package?

   _____   _____

6. How many packages would you have to buy if you wanted 30 in all?_____

Dividing with Basic Facts

Number Sentence

Use the numbers on the sign.

Use addition, subtraction, multiplication, or division.

Write two number sentences that are true.

Example
$30 \div 5 = 6$
$10 - 6 = 4$

| 10 | 5 |
| 30 | 6 |

1.

_____ = 28

_____ = 54

| 6 | 4 |
| 9 | 7 |

2.

_____ = 16

_____ = 3

| 18 | 7 |
| 9 | 6 |

3.

_____ = 7

_____ = 4

| 9 | 12 |
| 13 | 5 |

4.

_____ = 3

_____ = 11

| 24 | 8 |
| 7 | 4 |

5.

_____ = 0

_____ = 6

| 8 | 36 |
| 6 | 0 |

Get Four

Ask someone to play this game with you.

You need 2 number cubes and a pencil.

Take turns.

On each turn:

- Roll 2 number cubes.

- Add, subtract, or multiply the two numbers you roll.

- Write your initials in a square on the gameboard that shows the sum, difference, or product.

A square may have more than one player's initials.

The first player to initial four squares in the same row, column, or diagonal is the winner.

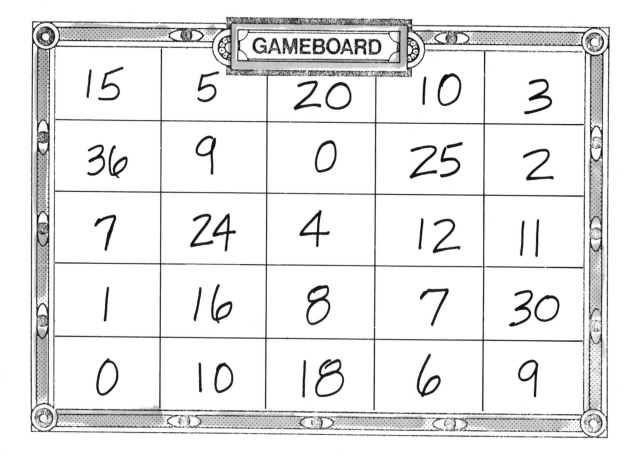

GAMEBOARD

15	5	20	10	3
36	9	0	25	2
7	24	4	12	11
1	16	8	7	30
0	10	18	6	9

Using Mixed Operations with Basic Facts

Cross Numbers

Use the operations +, —, ×, ÷.

Put an operation sign in each empty box.

Make true number sentences across and down.

1.

5		7	=	12
3		2	=	6
=		=		=
15		9	=	6

2.

18		6	=	3
2		4	=	8
=		=		=
9		2	=	11

3.

7		2	=	14
6		3	=	2
=		=		=
13		6	=	7

4.

24		3	=	8
6		2	=	3
=		=		=
4		1	=	5

Numbers Up

2, 3, or 4 people can play this game.

- Use cards.
  Make 10 number cards like these.

- Take turns.

- Mix up the cards and place them face down.

- Pick two cards.

- Use the numbers and +, −, × or ÷.
  Write a number sentence.

    If the answer is greater than 30, score 2 points.

    If the answer is less than 10, score 2 points.

    If the answer is between 10 and 30, score 1 point.

- Mix up the cards again before the next player's turn.

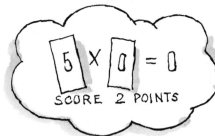

After six turns, the player with the highest score is the winner.

Players:				
Turn 1				
Turn 2				
Turn 3				
Turn 4				
Turn 5				
Turn 6				
Total Score				

Using Mixed Operations with Basic Facts

Big Numbers

Find the BIG NUMBER. Use the clues to help you.

1. Use 2, 3, 7, 8.
Clues:
- The 2 is in the ones place.
- The 7 is in the hundreds place.
- The 8 is in the tens place.
- The 3 is in the thousands place.

BIG NUMBER ☐☐☐☐

2. Use 5, 0, 9, 4.
Clues:
- The greatest number is in the tens place.
- The smallest number is in the ones place.
- The number in the thousands place is less than the number in the hundreds place.

BIG NUMBER ☐☐☐☐

3. Use 9, 5, 2, 8.
Clues:
- The greatest number is in the thousands place.
- The smallest number is in the ones place.
- The number in the hundreds place is greater than the number in the tens place.

BIG NUMBER ☐☐☐☐

4. Use 1, 6, 2, 7.
Clues:
- The number in the hundreds place is 4 more than the number in the tens place.
- The greatest number is in the ones place.

BIG NUMBER ☐☐☐☐

5. Use 3, 5, 6, 4.
Clues:
- The 5 is in the hundreds place.
- The sum of the numbers in the hundreds place and the ones place is nine.
- The number in the tens place is less than the number in the hundreds place.

BIG NUMBER ☐☐☐☐

6. Use 7, 1, 0, 9.
Clues:
- The number in the ones place is 6 more than the number in the hundreds place.
- The number in the thousands place is 9 more than the number in the tens place.

BIG NUMBER ☐☐☐☐

Place It Right

2, 3, or 4 people can play this game.

- Make 9 number cards like these.

- Mix up the cards and place them face down.

- Each player draws these boxes on a sheet of paper.

- Turn over one card.
  Each player writes the number in one of the boxes.

- Turn over another card.
  Each player writes the number in one of the boxes.

- Do this two more times.

- Compare the numbers.

  The player with the greatest number is the winner.

Challenge Question:

  Use the same four number cards. How many different numbers can you make? _____

  Show the numbers here.

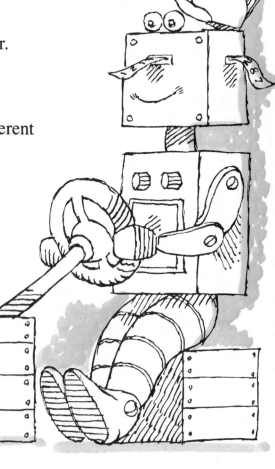

Tiny Toys

CAR $5.19

VAN $7.25

TAXI $8.79

TRUCK $13.99

DUNE BUGGY $16.29

BUS $11.80

Round each price to the nearest dollar.

Tell what each person bought.

1.
I bought one toy.
I spent about $12.
I bought a _____ .

2.
I bought two different toys.
I spent about $12.
I bought a _____ and
a _____ .

3.
I bought two different toys.
I spent about $30.
I bought a _____ and
a _____ .

4.
I bought two different toys.
I spent about $16.
I bought a _____ and
a _____ .

5.
I bought three different toys.
I spent about $42.
I bought a _____ and
a _____ and
a _____ .

6.
I bought three of the same toys.
I spent about $21.
I bought three _____ .

Rounding Bingo

Here's a game for you and your friend.

Rules

- Take turns.
- Pick two numbers from the sign.
- Round each number to the nearest hundred.
- Add the rounded numbers.
- Mark the answer on the game board.
  Use your **X** or **O**.

1,401	358
275	109
899	521

X_____   **O**_____

The first player with four **X**s or **O**s in a row, column, or diagonal is the winner.

GAMEBOARD

1,000	1,900	800	2,300
1,400	1,700	1,200	400
1,800	500	FREE	1,500
700	600	1,300	900

Tic-Tac-Sum

172	10
258	424
20	

Pick any two of these numbers.

Add the two numbers. Use the work space.

Put an **X** on the sum.

When you get three **X**s in a row, stop!

430	682	182
444	596	268
278	434	⌇192⌇

Work
Space

$$\begin{array}{r} 172 \\ + 20 \\ \hline 192 \end{array}$$

100	510
390	50
840	

Try again. Use these numbers.

Can you get three **X**s in a row with fewer tries?

440	940	1,230
610	900	560
890	1,350	490

Work
Space

The Largest-Smallest Trivia Quiz

Here's a quiz for you and your family.
First try to answer the question.
Then add.
Ring the sum. The sum gives the answer to the question.

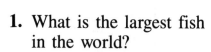

1. What is the largest fish
in the world?

102	cod	43
112	whale shark	+ 69
113	tuna	
1,012	sea bass	

2. What is the smallest
fish in the world?

1,843	guppy	1,564
1,743	goldfish	+ 289
1,753	angelfish	
1,853	goby	

3. What is the largest bird
in the world?

133	turkey	128
113	parrot	+ 15
161	penguin	
143	ostrich	

4. What is the smallest
bird in the world?

1,190	parakeet	505
1,290	robin	+ 695
1,200	Helena's hummingbird	
1,195	bluejay	

5. What is the largest dog
in the world?

616	St. Bernard	236
516	golden retriever	+ 380
556	collie	
510	Great Dane	

6. What is the smallest dog
in the world?

7,000	Yorkshire terrier	3,192
6,990	toy poodle	+ 3,808
6,900	chihuahua	
6,910	bull dog	

Adding 2- to 4-Digit Numbers

Cross-Number Puzzle

Subtract.
Write the differences in the cross-number puzzle.

ACROSS

1)　　338
　　 - 147

3)　　107
　　 - 62

4)　　803
　　 - 7

5)　　349
　　 - 296

6)　　98
　　 - 49

8)　　1,040
　　 - 168

12)　9,229
　　-3,179

13)　810
　　 - 381

DOWN

1)　6,284
　　-4,960

2)　937
　　 - 759

3)　7,821
　　-3,165

7)　9,930
　　 - 129

9)　92
　　 - 17

10)　803
　　 - 569

11)　719
　　 - 90

199

This is a game for you and a friend.
Each player starts with a score of 199.

Take turns.
On each turn:

■ Roll 1 or 2 number cubes.

■ Use the number cubes to make a number.

■ Subtract the number from your score.

■ If you make a number greater than
your score, you lose.

The first player to reach a score of zero is the winner.

Subtracting 2- to 4-Digit Numbers

Estimating Products

Pick a number from the cloud to make the sentence true.

1. $66 \times \boxed{}$ is between 100 and 200.

2. $31 \times \boxed{}$ is between 200 and 300.

3. $98 \times \boxed{}$ is between 700 and 800.

4. $27 \times \boxed{}$ is between 100 and 200.

5. $82 \times \boxed{}$ is between 500 and 600.

6. $43 \times \boxed{}$ is between 300 and 400.

Cloud 1: 1   5   7   3

Cloud 2: 2   6   8   4

Cloud 3: 4   5   6   8

Cloud 4: 9   3   5   2

Cloud 5: 7   4   9   5

Cloud 6: 5   3   6   9

Multiplication Puzzle

Find a friend who likes to solve puzzles.

Work together to make multiplication examples that are true.

Use each of the numbers on the sign.

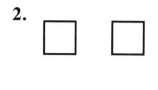

It may help to write the numbers on pieces of paper. Then you can move the numbers around until you place them correctly.

1.

$$
\begin{array}{r}
\square\ \square \\
\times\ \ \ 2 \\
\hline
\square\ \square
\end{array}
$$

6   8

3   4

2.

$$
\begin{array}{r}
\square\ \square \\
\times\ \ \ 3 \\
\hline
\square\ \square
\end{array}
$$

1   5

4   5

3.

$$
\begin{array}{r}
\square\ \square \\
\times\ \ \ 5 \\
\hline
\square\ \square
\end{array}
$$

4   0

1   6

4.

$$
\begin{array}{r}
\square\ \square \\
\times\ \ \ 3 \\
\hline
\square\ \square
\end{array}
$$

7   8

2   6

Multiplying 2-Digit Numbers by 1-Digit Numbers

Teeth Totals

Divide.

The answer gives you a fact about teeth.

The number of teeth a pig has

2) 88

2. The number of teeth a cat has

3) 90

The number of teeth an opossum has

1) 50

4. The number of teeth an adult human has

2) 64

The number of teeth a hedgehog has

2) 72

6. The number of teeth a dog has

2) 84

The number of teeth a kangaroo has

3) 96

8. The number of teeth a walrus has

5) 90

9. Which animal has the same number of teeth as an adult human? _____

10. Which animals have more teeth than an adult human? _____

_____

Divvy Up

Play Divvy Up with a friend.

You will need:

A playing board for each player.
You can draw the board on a sheet of paper.

9 number cards like these.

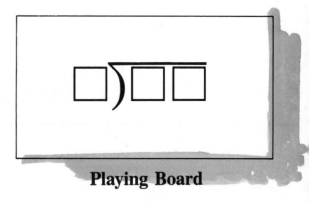

Playing Board

| 1 | 2 | 3 | 4 | 5 | 6 | 7 | 8 | 9 |

Here is how to play:

■ Mix the cards and place them face down in a pile.

■ Turn over one card.

■ Both you and your friend write the number in a box on your playing boards.

■ Turn over a second card. Write the number in a box.

■ Turn over a third card. Write the number in a box.

■ Divide.

The winner is the player with the greatest answer.

Draw another playing board and play again.

Dividing 2-Digit Numbers by 1-Digit Numbers

Arrow Path

Move around on the number board.

25↑ Means start at 25.
Move up one space.
You stop at 35.

43→ Means start at 43.
Move right one space.
You stop at 44.

6↑↑ Means start at 6.
Move up two spaces.
You stop at 26.

91	92	93	94	95	96	97	98	99	100
81	82	83	84	85	86	87	88	89	90
71	72	73	74	75	76	77	78	79	80
61	62	63	64	65	66	67	68	69	70
51	52	53	54	55	56	57	58	59	60
41	42	43	44	45	46	47	48	49	50
31	32	33	34	35	36	37	38	39	40
21	22	23	24	25	26	27	28	29	30
11	12	13	14	15	16	17	18	19	20
1	2	3	4	5	6	7	8	9	10

Write the missing numbers.

START	ARROWS	STOP
2	↑	
14	↑	
38	↑	
15	→	
31	→	
42	←	
57	←	
25	↓	
39	↓ →	
6	↑ ↑	
21	↓ → →	
80	↓ ↓ ↓ ←	
38	↑ ↑ ↑ →	

Write the missing arrows.

START	ARROWS	STOP
3		13
35		55
64		44
32		35
76		73
7		26
52		14
19		85
22		34
98		56
62		95
16		66
37		80

Magic Nines

Be a magician.

Cover your eyes.
Give these rules to an adult to follow.

■ Write down a three-digit number.

> 458
> is a three-
> digit number.

■ Use the same three digits to
write a different number.

> I can write
> 845.

■ Subtract the smaller number from
the greater number.

■ Add the digits in the difference.
Keep adding digits until you get just one.

> $$845$$
> $$- \ 458$$
> $$387$$
>
> $$3 + 8 + 7 = 18$$
> $$1 + 8 = 9$$

Now you say, "Abrakadabrah, mollickymine.
Your final answer is 9."

Try it again!

Using Number Patterns

Birthday Logic

October

Sunday	Monday	Tuesday	Wednesday	Thursday	Friday	Saturday
		1	2	3	4	5
6	7	8	9	10	11	12
13	14	15	16	17	18	19
20	21	22	23	24	25	26
27	28	29	30	31		

Use the calendar to help you find each person's birth date.

1. My birthday is on a Tuesday.
It is after October 2.
It is before October 14.
My birthday is October_____.

Karen

2. My birthday is on a Wednesday.
When you count by 5s you say
the number of my birth date.
My birthday is October_____.

Bob

3. My birthday is on a Tuesday.
My birthday is two weeks after
Karen's birthday.

My birthday is October_____.

Ted

4. My birthday is on a Sunday.
It is before Ted's birthday.
When you count by 3s you say
my birth date.
My birthday is October_____.

Carol

5. My birthday is on a weekend.
It is after Ted's birthday.
It is not a Sunday.
My birthday is October_____.

Sheila

6. My birthday is on a Monday.
The date is the number of days
in 3 weeks.
My birthday is October_____.

Dan

Seconds Count

Are you a good guesser?
  To check it out, you'll need a friend to time you.
  Your friend will need a watch or a timer that measures seconds.

Write down your guesses first.
Then do the tasks as your friend counts.
Fill in the count.

30-SECOND TASKS

How many times can you:	Guess	Count
clap your hands?		
tap your foot?		
jump up and down?		
write your telephone number?		

Draw a ring around your best guess.

60-SECOND TASKS

How many:	Guess	Count
animals can you name?		
foods can you name?		
states can you name?		
U.S. Presidents can you name?		

Draw a ring around your best guess.

Finding the Time

Measure Up

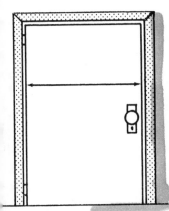

> A doorway is about 1 meter wide.

■ Make a list of five objects.
■ Cut a piece of string one meter long. Use the string to check each object.
■ Put an **X** in the box that tells about the length of each object.

Object	Length		
	About one meter	**More than one meter**	**Less then one meter**
1.			
2.			
3.			
4.			
5.			

Which object was closest to one meter long?_____

Now use the string to see how you measure up.

You	Length		
	About one meter	**More than one meter**	**Less than one meter**
6. Height			
7. Leg			
8. Arm span			
9. Walking step			

Fish Quiz

This is a quiz for you and your family.

1 meter = 100 centimeters

The lengths of the saltwater fish are on the sign.
Use each number once. Read the clues to find the lengths of the
fish in centimeters.

91	300
400	
61	340
160	
270	46

1. The sailfish is 3 meters long.
The sailfish is _____ centimeters long.

2. The Atlantic cod is 9 centimeters less than
one meter long. The Atlantic cod is
_____ centimeters long.

3. The great barracuda is 60 centimeters more
than one meter long. The great barracuda
is _____ centimeters long.

4. The bluefin tuna is
2 meters 70 centimeters long.
The bluefin tuna is _____ centimeters long.

5. The ocean sunfish is 3 meters 40 centimeters
long. The ocean sunfish is _____ centimeters
long.

6. The swordfish is 1 meter longer than
the sailfish. The swordfish is
_____ centimeters long.

7. The bluefish is 11 centimeters more than
half a meter long. The bluefish is
_____ centimeters long.

8. The black sea bass is 4 centimeters less
than half a meter long. The black sea
bass is _____ centimeters long.

Measurement Sense

Use each unit in the sign once. Make sure the measurements make sense.

inches		pounds
	ounces	hours
quart		days
	miles	feet
years		minutes

1. Marcie is 9 _____ old.

2. She is 50 _____ tall and weighs 56 _____ .

3. Her brother, Paul, is 4 _____ tall.

4. Paul is 365 _____ younger than Marcie.

5. Marcie drinks 8 _____ of orange juice each morning and 1 _____ of milk every day.

6. Marcie and Paul ride their bicycles 2 _____ to school.

7. It takes them about 15 _____ to ride to school.

8. They go to school for 6 _____ each day.

Measures In
The Kitchen

Take a look in your kitchen or in a store.

Ask an adult to help you.

1. What can you find that is measured in pounds? _____
   How many pounds?

_____   _____   _____

2. What can you find that is measured in ounces? _____

   How many ounces?

_____   _____   _____

3. What can you find that is measured in quarts? _____
   How many quarts?

_____   _____   _____

4. What can you find that is measured in gallons? _____
   How many gallons?

_____   _____   _____

Graph Pictures

Graph each point.

Connect the points in order.

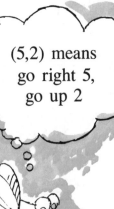

(5,2) means
go right 5,
go up 2

1. (5,2)
2. (3,3)
3. (4,4)
4. (2,7)
5. (4,8)
6. (2,9)
7. (3,10)
8. (2,14)
9. (4,13)
10. (3,14)
11. (4,15)
12. (3,16)
13. (4,17)
14. (3,18)
15. (4,18)
16. (4,19)
17. (6,18)
18. (7,19)
19. (7,18)
20. (11,15)
21. (10,15)
22. (10,14)
23. (7,15)
24. (8,14)
25. (10,12)
26. (10,9)
27. (9,7)

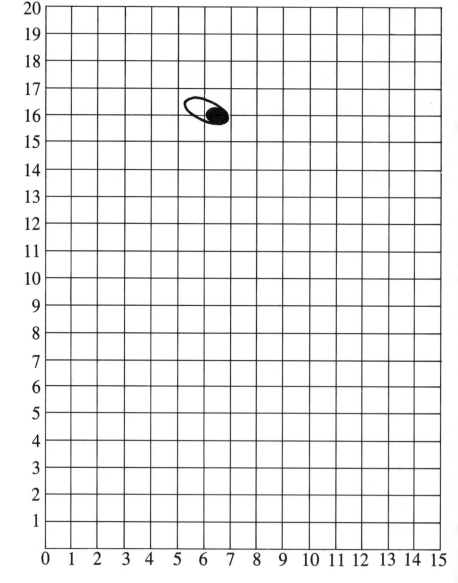

28. (8,6)
29. (8,4)

30. (9,3)
31. (11,3)

32. (12,4)
33. (11,5)

34. (12,5)
35. (13,4)

36. (10,1)
37. (5,2)

The (12,12) Race

Ask someone to play this game with you.
You need a number cube and 2 markers.

- Each player begins at (0, 0).

- Take turns.

- On each turn:
    Roll the number cube two times.
    The first roll tells the number of spaces to move right.
    The second roll tells the number of spaces to move up.

When you are in the shaded area:
    Roll the number cube only once.
    You may choose to move right or up.
If you cannot move the number of spaces rolled,
    you lose your turn.

The winner is the first player to reach (12,12).

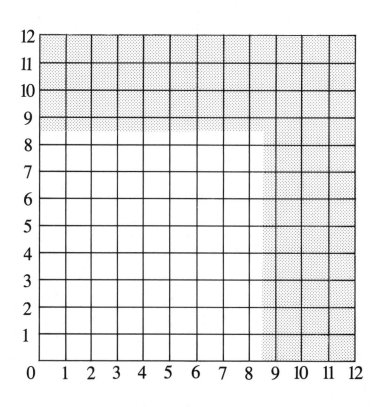

Mirror Image

Hold the edge of a mirror on the vertical lines in these letters.

1. Look in the mirror. Describe what you see.

_____

Each of these letters has a vertical line of **symmetry.**

2. Name some other capital letters with vertical lines

of symmetry. _____

3. Write a word in which every letter has a vertical line

of symmetry. _____

Hold the edge of a mirror on the horizontal lines in these letters.

4. Look in the mirror. Describe what you see. _____

_____

Each of these letters has a horizontal line of symmetry.

5. Name some other capital letters with horizonal lines

of symmetry. _____

6. Write a word in which every letter has a horizontal line

of symmetry. _____

Face Symmetry

Find a magazine with pictures.
Ask an adult to help you.

- Cut out a picture of a face.
- Cut the face in half vertically.
- Paste half of the face on this paper.
- Draw the other side of the face yourself.

Shape Cents

Here are the prices.

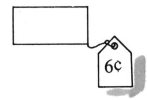 6¢   4¢   1¢   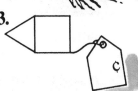 3¢

EXAMPLE

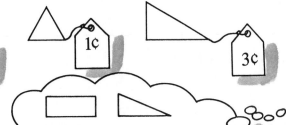

6¢ + 3¢ = 9¢

How much are these?

1.

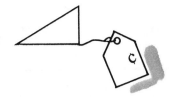

2.

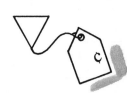

3.

4.

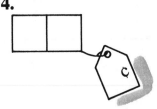

5.

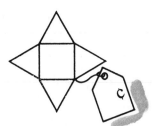

6.

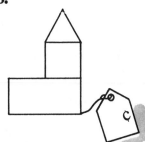

7.

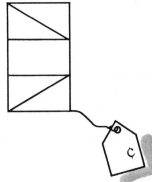

8.

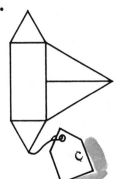

9.

Hidden Shapes

This is a hidden quiz for you and your family.

Read the clue.

Use the letters as corners.

Connect the letters to make the shape, and fill in the blank.

I am a rectangle and a drink.

I am ___MILK___ .

M . K . R .

I . L . Q .

---

1. I am a triangle and a color.

I am _____ .

R . O . L .

E . D . M .

---

2. I am a triangle and an animal.

I am _____ .

S . M . A .

P . C . T .

---

3. I am a rectangle and a flower.

I am _____ .

M . S . R .

A . O . E .

---

4. I am a rectangle and a coin.

I am _____ .

D . N . I . P .

M . L . E . Y .

---

5. I am a square and a boy's name.

I am _____ .

J . N . R . D .

O . H . A . T .

---

6. I am a square and a piece of fruit.

I am _____ .

O . P . E . G .

L . A . R .

Riddle Stumpers

HOW ARE A KING AND A METER STICK ALIKE?

Write the letter of the square on the line above the fraction that tells what part of the square is shaded.

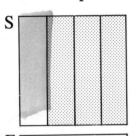
S

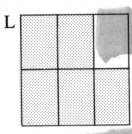
L

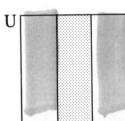
U

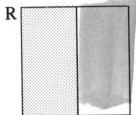
E

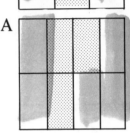
R

A

THEY BOTH ____ ____ ____   ____ ____ ____ ____ ____ ____

$\frac{3}{8}$ $\frac{1}{2}$ $\frac{2}{3}$ $\frac{1}{2}$ $\frac{1}{3}$ $\frac{5}{6}$ $\frac{2}{3}$ $\frac{1}{2}$ $\frac{3}{4}$

HOW ARE A WRITER AND A PIG ALIKE?

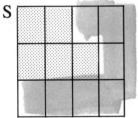
S

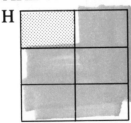
H

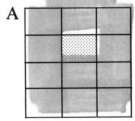
A

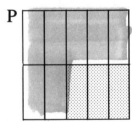
P

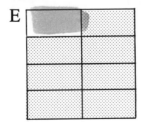
V

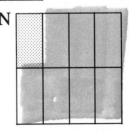
E

N

THEY BOTH ____ ____ ____ ____   ____ ____ ____ ____

$\frac{1}{6}$ $\frac{1}{12}$ $\frac{1}{4}$ $\frac{7}{8}$ $\frac{3}{10}$ $\frac{7}{8}$ $\frac{1}{8}$ $\frac{5}{12}$

Color-In

Play this game with a friend.

You will need two different colored crayons or markers.

Rules

■ Take turns.

■ On a turn, color in a total of $\frac{1}{8}$, $\frac{2}{8}$ or $\frac{3}{8}$ of a square.

For example, if you choose $\frac{2}{8}$
you may color $\frac{2}{8}$ of one square
or $\frac{1}{8}$ of one square and $\frac{1}{8}$ of another square.

The player who colors the last region is the winner.

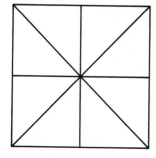
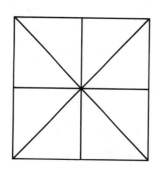

Part of a Group

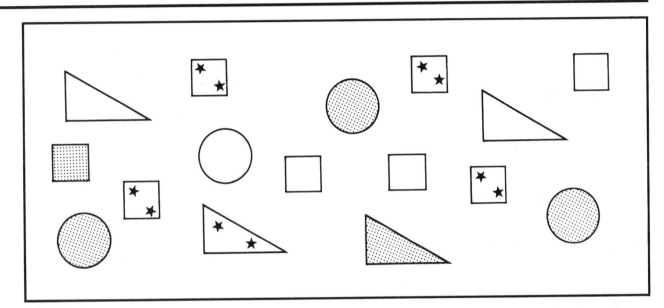

Make true sentences about the picture.

Write **circles**, **triangles**, or **squares**.

1. $\frac{3}{4}$ of the _____ are shaded.

2. $\frac{3}{8}$ of the _____ are plain.

3. $\frac{0}{4}$ of the _____ have stars.

4. $\frac{1}{4}$ of the _____ are shaded.

5. $\frac{2}{4}$ of the _____ are plain.

6. $\frac{4}{8}$ of the _____ have stars.

Finding Fractional Parts of a Set

Fraction Code

HOW ARE A FISH AND A PIANO ALIKE?

Solve this riddle with a friend.
Use the fraction code to find the answer.
Write the letters in the boxes in order.

1. The first $\frac{1}{4}$ of TOAD.

2. The first $\frac{2}{4}$ of HEAT.

3. The first $\frac{1}{3}$ of YOU.

4. The first $\frac{2}{5}$ of BOARD.

5. The first $\frac{2}{4}$ of THAT.

6. The first $\frac{2}{3}$ of HAD.

7. The first $\frac{3}{4}$ of VEST.

8. The first $\frac{3}{7}$ of CALLING.

9. The last $\frac{2}{5}$ of DATES.

T			

Finding Fractional Parts of a Set

Fraction Shapes

Connect fractions
equivalent to $\frac{1}{2}$
to make a rectangle.

$\frac{1}{5}$ $\frac{6}{12}$ $\frac{3}{9}$ $\frac{2}{4}$

$\frac{2}{3}$ $\frac{5}{10}$ $\frac{7}{12}$ $\frac{3}{6}$

Connect fractions
equivalent to $\frac{1}{3}$
to make a kite.

$\frac{3}{4}$ $\frac{2}{6}$ $\frac{1}{9}$

$\frac{5}{15}$ $\frac{1}{8}$ $\frac{4}{12}$

$\frac{6}{12}$ $\frac{3}{9}$ $\frac{3}{6}$

Connect fractions
equivalent to $\frac{1}{4}$
to make a triangle.

$\frac{4}{16}$ $\frac{4}{8}$ $\frac{3}{12}$

$\frac{2}{4}$ $\frac{2}{8}$ $\frac{4}{12}$

Connect fractions
equivalent to $\frac{2}{3}$
to make a square.

$\frac{4}{6}$ $\frac{8}{12}$

$\frac{8}{10}$ $\frac{4}{9}$

$\frac{3}{9}$

$\frac{2}{9}$ $\frac{5}{9}$ $\frac{6}{12}$

$\frac{10}{15}$ $\frac{6}{9}$

A Capital Quiz

This is a quiz for you and your family.
How many state capitals do you know?
  Guess first.
  Then draw lines and match equivalent fractions
to check your guesses.

State	Capital
1. Montana $\frac{2}{3}$	$\frac{3}{15}$ Boston
2. Georgia $\frac{1}{2}$	$\frac{10}{12}$ Dover
3. Massachusetts $\frac{1}{5}$	$\frac{3}{9}$ Columbia
4. Ohio $\frac{3}{4}$	$\frac{2}{16}$ Denver
5. Alaska $\frac{2}{5}$	$\frac{2}{12}$ Austin
6. Texas $\frac{1}{6}$	$\frac{4}{6}$ Helena
7. South Carolina $\frac{1}{3}$	$\frac{4}{10}$ Juneau
8. Colorado $\frac{1}{8}$	$\frac{9}{12}$ Columbus
9. California $\frac{1}{4}$	$\frac{6}{12}$ Atlanta
10. Delaware $\frac{5}{6}$	$\frac{2}{8}$ Sacramento

Finding Equivalent Fractions

Mystery Number

Write the number for each word name.
Cross off the number in the cloud.
The number that is left is the mystery number.

25.1	47.82	14.02	9.36	6.9
20.01	5.7	60.43	70.05	5.07	20.10
15.04	8.7	10.1	8.17	14.2

1. five and seven tenths _____

2. six and nine tenths _____

3. fourteen and two tenths _____

4. twenty-five and one tenth _____

5. eight and seventeen hundredths _____

6. nine and thirty-six hundredths _____

7. fifteen and four hundredths _____

8. forty-seven and eighty-two hundredths _____

9. eight and seven tenths _____

10. sixty and forty-three hundredths _____

11. seventy and five hundredths _____

12. fourteen and two hundredths _____

13. five and seven hundredths _____

14. ten and one tenth _____

15. twenty and ten hundredths _____

THE MYSTERY NUMBER IS _____

Sports Facts

This is a sports trivia quiz for you and your family.
First try to answer the questions.
Then check by matching the word name with the number.
The number gives the answer to the question. Ring the
correct answer.

1. Four and six tenths

How many rings are on the Olympic flag?
4.6   There is 1 ring.
4.06   There are 3 rings.
4.6   There are 5 rings.
0.46   There are 7 rings.

2. Three and eleven hundredths

How many pins are in the back row of bowling?
3.11   There are 4 pins.
31.1   There are 5 pins.
311   There are 8 pins.
0.311   There are 10 pins.

3. Six and eight hundredths

What is the distance between bases on a baseball diamond?
6.8   The distance is 100 feet.
6.08   The distance is 90 feet.
0.68   The distance is 60 feet.
68   The distance is 50 feet.

4. Twelve and one tenth

How many yards long is a football field from goal post to
goal post?
1.21   The field is 100 yards long.
121   The field is 300 yards long.
12.1   The field is 120 yards long.
0.121   The field is 150 yards long.

5. Forty and two hundredths

Who holds the lifetime record for batting the most
homeruns?
402   Lou Gehrig
4.02   Willie Mays
40.2   Babe Ruth
40.02   Hank Aaron

Finding Decimals to Hundredths

Decimal Locksmith

The number on the lock is the target number.
Put an **X** on the two keys with numbers whose sum or difference
is the target number.

1.

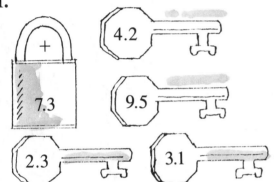

2.

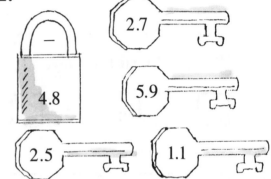

3.

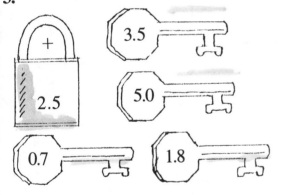

4.

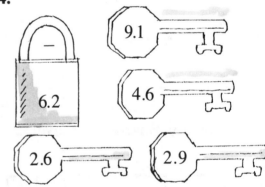

5.

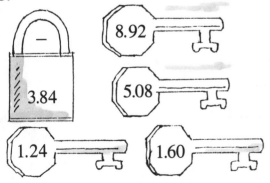

6.

Decimal Play-offs

Ask someone to play this game with you.
You need 1 number cube and 2 pencils.

- Take turns.

- Roll the number cube.
  Write the number in one of the squares on your playing board.

- After the squares are filled in, add across.
  Then add to find the total.

The winner is the player with the greater total.

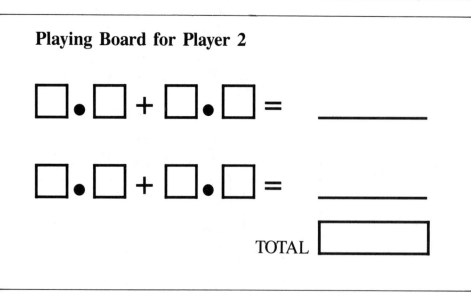

Playing Board for Player 1

$$\square . \square + \square . \square = \underline{\hspace{2cm}}$$

$$\square . \square + \square . \square = \underline{\hspace{2cm}}$$

TOTAL $\boxed{}$

Playing Board for Player 2

$$\square . \square + \square . \square = \underline{\hspace{2cm}}$$

$$\square . \square + \square . \square = \underline{\hspace{2cm}}$$

TOTAL $\boxed{}$

Adding and Subtracting Decimals

Collections of Money

Six children emptied their pockets.
The pictures show the coins they have.
Tell how much money each child has.

1. Brett said, "I do not have any quarters." Brett has _____ ¢.

2. Juan said, "All of my coins are different." Juan has _____ ¢.

3. Maria said, "I have more than one quarter." Maria has _____ ¢.

4. Carla said, "I do not have any pennies." Carla has _____ ¢.

5. Jason said, "I have four nickels." Jason has _____ ¢.

6. Lisa said, "I have more pennies than nickels." Lisa has _____ ¢.

Money Bags

Ask an adult to help you with this activity.
You need a paper bag and some coins.
Try to use at least 1 quarter, 1 dime, 1 nickel, and 1 penny.

- Put the coins in the paper bag.

- Close your eyes.

- Shake the bag.

- Reach in the bag and take a coin.

Can you tell the value of the coin by feeling it?

Open your eyes and check your guess.

Try again.

Using Money

Baseball Stars

The table shows the number of home runs made by some baseball players in their careers.

Home Run Leaders

Player	Number of Home Runs
Hank Aaron	755
Reggie Jackson	548
Harmon Killebrew	573
Mickey Mantle	536
Willie Mays	660
Frank Robinson	586
Babe Ruth	714

Use the information in the table to answer these questions.

1. How many home runs did Babe Ruth score?

_____

2. How many home runs did Reggie Jackson score?

_____

3. Who scored more home runs, Frank Robinson or Mickey Mantle?

_____

4. Who scored the greatest number of home runs?

_____

5. How many more home runs did Willie Mays score than Harmon Killebrew?

_____

6. How many more home runs did Babe Ruth score than Reggie Jackson?

_____

What Color Cars Go By?

Ask an adult to help you.

Watch 25 cars go by. Make a tally mark for the color of each car.

Color	
Black	
Blue	
Green	
Grey	
Red	
White	
Yellow	

Use the tally marks to make a table.

- Write the name of each color.

- Write the total number of cars for each color.

1. The greatest number of cars are the color _____ .

2. The least number of cars are the color _____ .

Color of Cars

Color	Number of Cars

Making a Table

Sam's Super Sandwiches

The bar graph shows what sandwiches Sam sold in one month.

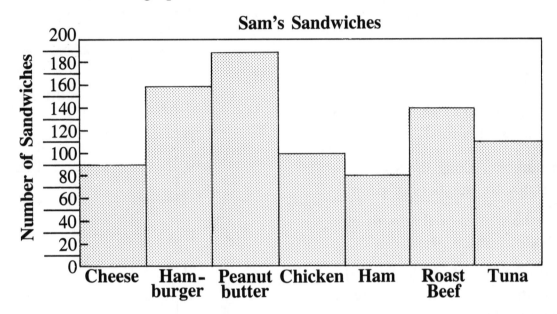

Use the information in the bar graph to fill in the numbers in these sentences.

1. Sam sold _____ roast beef sandwiches.
He sold _____ cheese sandwiches.
He sold _____ chicken sandwiches.

2. Sam sold _____ hamburger sandwiches.
He sold _____ more hamburger sandwiches than chicken sandwiches.

3. Sam sold _____ tuna sandwiches.
He sold _____ more tuna sandwiches than ham sandwiches.

4. Sam sold _____ peanut butter sandwiches.
He sold _____ more peanut butter sandwiches than cheese sandwiches.

Peanut Butter And ?

Conduct a **survey**.

- Ask 20 people to tell which of these foods they like best with peanut butter.

- Make a tally for each choice.

Foods

Jelly
Apple
Banana
Marshmallow
Pickles

Make a bar graph to show how many people chose each food.

- The numbers along the side of the graph are numbers of people.

- Write the names of the foods along the bottom of the graph.

- For each food, shade in a bar that shows the number of people who chose that food.

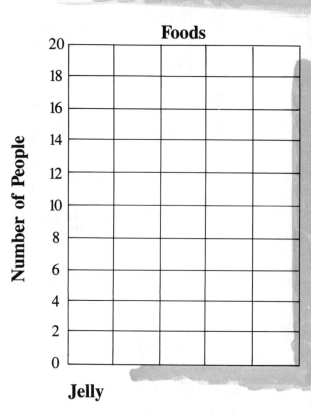

The greatest number of people like peanut butter and _____ .

Secret Codes

Use the clues to find each person's secret code.

2,136	9,822	6,847
4,346	3,346	2,946

1. Mia

My code has
a 7 in the ones
place. My code is

_____.

2. Kim

The sum of the
digits in my code
is 16. My code is

_____.

3. Bob

My code has an 8
in the hundreds
place. My code is

_____.

4. Ronald

My code has a 2
in the thousands
place. My code is

_____.

5. Tanya

My code is
less than Ronald's
code. My code is

_____.

6. Tony

My code is
greater than Kim's
code. My code is

_____.

The Between Game

Play this game with a friend.

One player is the **thinker**.
The thinker thinks of a mystery number between 1 and 500.

The other player is the **guesser**.
The guesser tries to guess the mystery number by asking "between" questions.

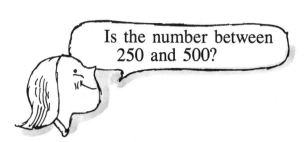

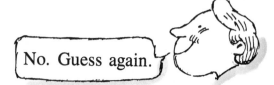

When the guesser knows the mystery number, the guesser says, **"The mystery number is . . ."**

Keep track of the number of questions.

1. What was the mystery number? _____

2. How many questions did you ask? _____

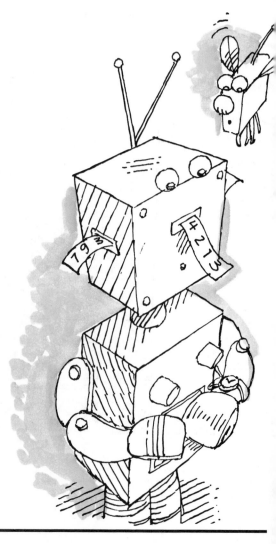

Using Logical Reasoning

Make Sense

Use the numbers on the signs to finish these stories.
Be sure that the numbers you choose make sense in the stories.

1. Sandy likes to play checkers with her mother.
They played _____ games. Sandy won
more games than her mother. Sandy won
_____ games. Her mother won _____ games.

7	4
	11

2. Tom went bowling. He scored _____ points
in the first game. He scored 20 more points in
the second game than in the first game. Tom
scored _____ points in the second game.
Tom scored a total of _____ points in the
two games.

110	
	90
	200

3. Jane played a ring toss game. She scored the
most points in the first game. She scored _____
points in the first game. She scored 10 points less
in the second game. Jane scored _____ points
in the second game. She scored _____ points
in the third game.

50	
	60
	58

4. Sandy, Tom and Jane played beanbag toss. Sandy
scored _____ points. Tom scored twice as many
points as Sandy. Tom scored _____ points.
Jane scored 2 points less than Tom. Jane scored
_____ points.

	20
40	
	38

Game Facts

Find some people who like to play games.
Work together to fill in the numbers.
The numbers must fit the facts about the game.

1. The game of checkers is a game for _____ players.
At the beginning of the game, each player has
_____ checkers. Altogether, there are _____
checkers.

> 2
>
> 12   24

2. Checkers is played on a square board that has
_____ sides. There are 8 rows of small squares
on the board. There are _____ small squares
in each row. Altogether, there are _____ small
squares on a checkerboard.

> 64
>
> 8   4

3. The game of Monopoly was invented in _____ .
There are _____ railroads on the Monopoly board.
There are _____ places to land on the board.

> 40
> 1933
> 4

4. Monopoly players use play money. At the beginning
of a game, each player gets a total of $ _____ .
Players use their money to buy property. The
most expensive property is Boardwalk. It costs
$ _____ . Boardwalk costs $50 more than Park
Place. Park Place costs $ _____ .

> 350
> 400
> 1,500

Shopping Questions

Write a question for each story.
Then use the facts in the story to answer the question.

Mrs. Green bought 3 pairs of sunglasses
for $5 each. She bought an umbrella for $9.

Millie wrote:
How much more did the umbrella
cost than one pair of sunglasses?

$$\begin{array}{r} 9 \\ -\ 5 \\ \hline 4 \end{array}$$

The umbrella cost $4 more.

Eric wrote:
How much did Mrs. Green spend in all?

$$\begin{array}{r} 5 \\ \times\ 3 \\ \hline 15 \end{array} \qquad \begin{array}{r} 15 \\ +\ 9 \\ \hline 24 \end{array}$$

Mrs. Green spent $24 in all.

1. Bob bought 3 pounds of bananas for $.99. He also bought a cantelope for $.79.

2. Ann had $8.00. She bought a hat for $4.00. She bought a scarf for $2.75.

3. Dr. Hart bought a sweater for $29, a shirt for $21, and a tie for $18.

4. Mrs. Grady gave $8 to Sue and $8 to Jeff. Sue bought stickers for $2.00.

5. Todd bought 2 boxes of muffins for $1.20 each. One box had 12 bran muffins. The other box had 6 blueberry muffins.

6. Sandy bought 2 dozen flowers. Ten of the flowers were mums. Eight of the flowers were carnations. The rest of the flowers were roses.

Oodles Of Questions

2 or 3 people can play this game.

Set a time limit of 3 minutes for each story.

Each player should:
- Write lots of questions for each story.
- Answer the questions.
- Check the answers with the other players.
- Score 1 point for each question with a right answer.

The player with the greatest number of points for the four stories is the winner.

1. There are 26 bones in each of your feet. There are 27 bones in each hand. There are a total of 206 bones in your body.

2. A raw carrot has 21 calories. A stalk of celery has 5 calories. A medium green pepper has three times as many calories as a stalk of celery.

3. A dollar bill is about 16 centimeters long. It is about 7 centimeters wide. A dollar bill costs about 1¢ to produce.

4. A crab has 10 legs. A spider has 8 legs. An ant has 4 less legs than a crab.

Make It Even

Draw a line through each sign.
The total amount of money on each
side of the line must be the same.

1.

2.

3.

4.

Money In The Jar

Work with a friend.

Write the value of a coin in each circle to make the totals correct.

1.

2.

3.

4.

5.

6.

More. . .
he Between Game

this game with a friend.

player is the **thinker**.
thinker thinks of a mystery number between 1 and 500.

other player is the **guesser**.
guesser tries to guess the mystery number by asking "between"
tions.

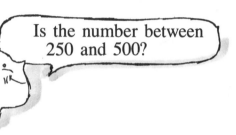

Is the number between
250 and 500?

No. Guess again.

en the guesser knows the mystery number,
guesser says, **"The mystery number is . . ."**

p track of the number of questions.

. What was the mystery number? _____

. How many questions did you ask? _____

p track of the number of questions.

. What was the mystery number? _____

. How many questions did you ask? _____

p track of the number of questions.

. What was the mystery number? _____

. How many questions did you ask? _____

Enrichment
Math Grade 4

AMERICAN
EDUCATION
PUBLISHING

Bead Cents

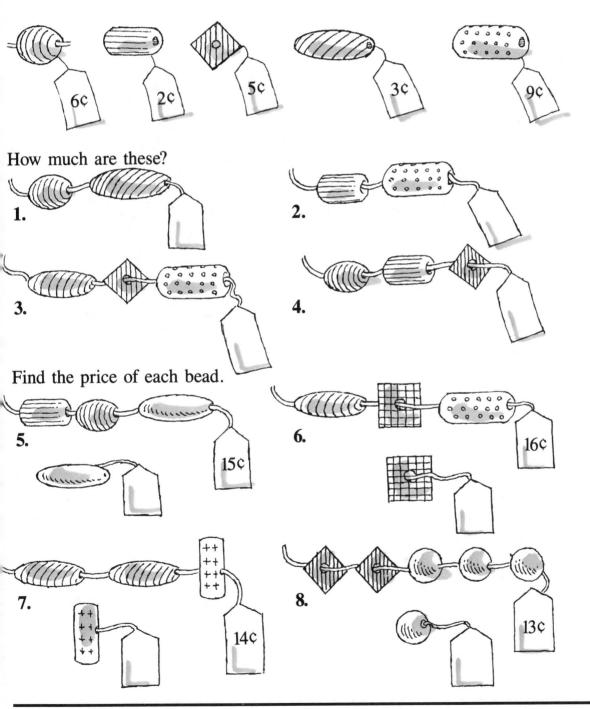

Here are the prices.

6¢   2¢   5¢   3¢   9¢

How much are these?

1.

2.

3.

4.

Find the price of each bead.

5.   15¢

6.   16¢

7.   14¢

8.   13¢

Middle of the Path

Ask someone to play this game with you.

You need two markers and ten number cards.

Number the cards 0-9.

Player 1 starts at 0.

Player 2 starts at 12.

Take turns.

   On each turn:

■ Pick a number card.

■ Add the number on the card to the number that your marker is on.

OR

■ Subtract the number on the card from the number that your marker is on.

■ Move your marker to the answer.

The first player to land on 6 is the winner.

You must move on each turn.

Your marker cannot leave the path.

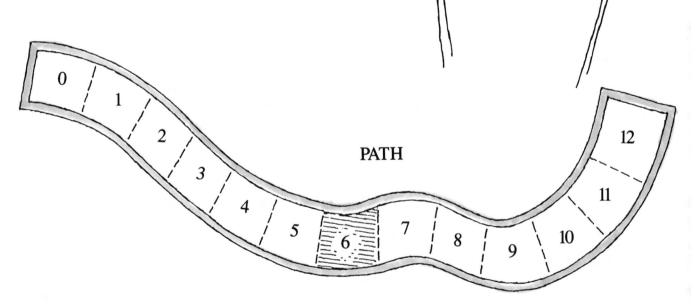

Who's Who?

Guess first.

Then multiply or divide.

Write the letter on the line above the answer.

1.   **WHO DEVELOPED A CODE FOR HELPING BLIND PEOPLE READ AND WRITE?**

___ ___ ___ ___ ___   ___ ___ ___ ___ ___ ___ ___
2   9   12   16   21   32   36   42   49   54   56   64

O	$3 \times 3 =$		L	$9 \times 6 =$
R	$4 \times 9 =$		I	$7 \times 7 =$
A	$6 \times 7 =$		L	$7 \times 8 =$
L	$2 \times 1 =$		B	$8 \times 4 =$
E	$8 \times 8 =$		U	$6 \times 2 =$
I	$4 \times 4 =$		S	$3 \times 7 =$

2.   **WHO WAS THE FIRST AMERICAN ASTRONAUT TO ORBIT THE EARTH?**

___ ___ ___ ___   ___ ___ ___ ___ ___
1   2   3   4   5   6   7   8   9

H	$15 \div 5 =$		N	$27 \div 3 =$
L	$24 \div 4 =$		G	$10 \div 2 =$
O	$18 \div 9 =$		N	$8 \div 1 =$
N	$28 \div 7 =$		J	$6 \div 6 =$
E	$56 \div 8 =$			

Follow the Path

Work together with a friend.

Take turns working each problem.

Fill in numbers to complete the paths.

Start   **End**

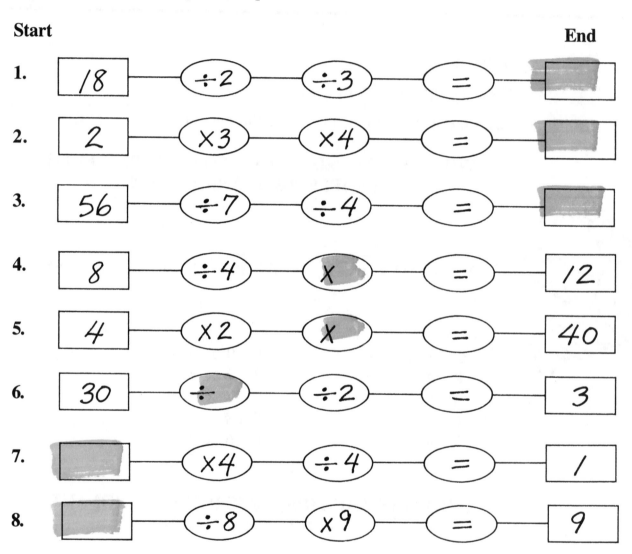

1. $18 \div 2 \div 3 =$ ▢

2. $2 \times 3 \times 4 =$ ▢

3. $56 \div 7 \div 4 =$ ▢

4. $8 \div 4 \times$ ▢ $= 12$

5. $4 \times 2 \times$ ▢ $= 40$

6. $30 \div$ ▢ $\div 2 = 3$

7. ▢ $\times 4 \div 4 = 1$

8. ▢ $\div 8 \times 9 = 9$

Multiplying and Dividing with Basic Facts

Detective Math

Read the clues.

Ring the two numbers on the sign that fit the clues.

1.
8	9
6	7

The sum is 15.
The difference is 1.

2.
6	9
2	3

The quotient is 3.
The product is 27.

3.
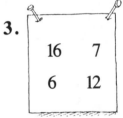
16	7
6	12

The difference is 9.
The quotient is 4.

4.
8	6
4	3

The product is 24.
The sum is 10.

5.
6	6
9	4

The quotient is 1.
The difference is 0.

6.
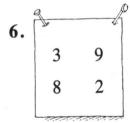
3	9
8	2

The sum is 11.
The difference is 5.

7.
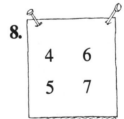
7	5
8	6

The sum is 13.
The difference is 1.

8.
4	6
5	7

The difference is 2
The product is 35.

9.
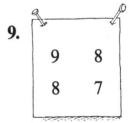
9	8
8	7

The product is 64.
The quotient is 1.

Number Match

Number Match is a game for 2 players.

You need 1 number cube.

- Take turns.

- Roll the number cube.

- Write the number in one of the boxes on the game sheet. You must make true number sentences. If you cannot use the number you roll, you lose a turn.

- The first player to fill in all of the boxes is the winner.

Game Sheet

Player 1: _____

$$\square \; + \; \square \; = \; 9$$
$$\square \; + \; \square \; > \; 10$$
$$\square \; - \; \square \; = \; 3$$
$$\square \; - \; \square \; < \; 4$$
$$\square \; \times \; \square \; = \; 20$$
$$\square \; \times \; \square \; > \; 24$$

Player 2: _____

$$\square \; + \; \square \; = \; 9$$
$$\square \; + \; \square \; > \; 10$$
$$\square \; - \; \square \; = \; 3$$
$$\square \; - \; \square \; < \; 4$$
$$\square \; \times \; \square \; = \; 20$$
$$\square \; \times \; \square \; > \; 24$$

Missing Numbers

Use these numbers.
Put one number in the correct box below.

Cross off the number after you use it.

13	27		8	9	
18	6				0
36	12	1		7	17
2	5	3	14		

1.
```
    1
-  □
───
   0
```

2.
```
   9
 +9
───
 □
```

3.
```
   4
 ×3
───
 □
```

4.
```
  □
6)18
```

5.
```
   6
 ×6
───
 □
```

6.
```
  □
 -8
───
  5
```

7.
```
  □
4)0
```

8.
```
  □
 +6
───
 13
```

9.
```
   4
+ □
───
 13
```

10.
```
   1
□)2
```

11.
```
 □
×5
───
40
```

12.
```
  □
 -8
───
  9
```

13.
```
   9
3)□
```

14.
```
   7
 +7
───
  □
```

15.
```
  11
- □
───
  6
```

16.
```
   9
× □
───
 54
```

Two's and Three's

Work with a friend.

■ Use 2s and 3s with +, −, ×, or ÷.

■ Write true number sentences.

Each sentence must have *at least* one 2 and one 3.

1. _____ = 0

2. _____ = 1

3. _____ = 2

4. _____ = 3

5. _____ = 4

6. _____ = 5

7. _____ = 6

8. _____ = 7

9. _____ = 8

10. _____ = 9

$3 - 2 = 1$

$3 \div 3 + 2 - 2 = 1$

$(3 + 2) \div (3 + 2) = 1$

$2 \div 2 \times 3 \div 3 = 1$

Using Mixed Operations with Basic Facts

Cross-Number Puzzle

LESSON
5

Write the number in the cross-number puzzle.

ACROSS

1. Three hundred twenty-six thousand, three hundred forty-five

5. Fifty thousand, three hundred twenty-six

7. Forty-three ·

8. Thirty-three

10. Nine hundred four

11. Twenty-one

12. Seventy-one thousand, thirty-two

13. Three hundred ninety-five

14. Four thousand, eight hundred fifty-six

DOWN

2. Three hundred thirty thousand, one

3. Three thousand, twenty-four

4. Eight hundred ninety-three

6. Six hundred thirty-two thousand, one hundred eighty-four

9. Thirty-eight thousand, two hundred fifty-six

10. Nine thousand, two hundred seventy-three

Digit Derby

Make these number cards.
Find 2 markers.
Ask someone at home to play this game with you.

$$0 \quad 1 \quad 2 \quad 3 \quad 4 \quad 5 \quad 6 \quad 7 \quad 8 \quad 9$$

Mix up the cards and place them face down.

Place the markers in any two squares on the game board.

Take turns.

Game Board

183,426	507,932	391,706
231,849	762,045	918,620
456,195	329,607	584,371
970,584	618,390	842,753

On each turn:
- Pick a card.
- Move the marker one space horizontally, vertically, or diagonally to a number that has the digit on the card.

Score:
- 6 points if the digit is in the hundred thousands place.
- 5 points if the digit is in the ten thousands place.
- 4 points if the digit is in the thousands place.
- 3 points if the digit is in the hundreds place.
- 2 points if the digit is in the tens place.
- 1 point if the digit is in the ones place.

After every card has been picked, find the total of the scores. The winner is the player with the greater total score.

Score Sheet

	Player 1:	Player 2:
Turn 1		
Turn 2		
Turn 3		
Turn 4		
Turn 5		
TOTAL		

Using Place Value to Hundred Thousands

Forming Numbers

Fill in the missing digit.

The number must fit the fact.

1. ____ 8 8 9
Rounded to the nearest
thousand, the number is
4,000.

2. ____ 1 6 3
Rounded to the nearest
thousand, the number is
5,000.

3. ____ 4 9 9
Rounded to the nearest
thousand, the number is
9,000.

4. ____ 5 2 7
Rounded to the nearest
thousand, the number is
2,000.

5. 1 ____ 4 9 7
Rounded to the nearest
thousand, the number is
13,000.

6. 5 ____ 0 0 1
Rounded to the nearest
thousand, the number is
56,000.

7. 6 ____ 8 6 2
Rounded to the nearest
thousand, the number is
61,000.

8. 8 ____ 5 0 0
Rounded to the nearest
thousand, the number is
90,000.

Use the digits to form numbers.

9. Use 3, 5, 7, 8 .

____ ____ ____ ____

Rounded to the nearest
thousand, the number is
7,000.

10. Use 1, 2, 6, 8 .

____ ____ ____ ____

Rounded to the nearest
thousand, the number is
7,000.

Roll and Round

Play this game with a friend.

To Play:

- One player rolls a number cube.

- Both players write the number in one of the boxes on their score sheets.

- After all 16 boxes are filled, players round each number to the nearest thousand.

- Players compare the four rounded numbers, one for one.

To Score:

- Score 1 point for the greater rounded number.

- Score 0 for a tie.

The player with the greater total score is the winner.

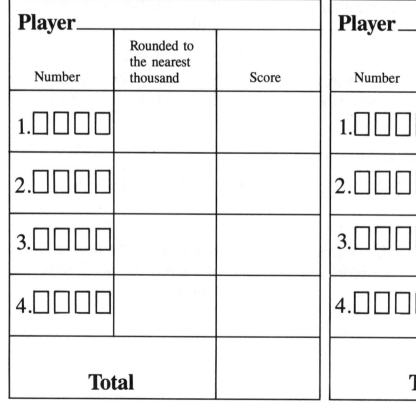

Player_____		
Number	Rounded to the nearest thousand	Score
1.☐☐☐☐		
2.☐☐☐☐		
3.☐☐☐☐		
4.☐☐☐☐		
Total		

Player_____		
Number	Rounded to the nearest thousand	Score
1.☐☐☐☐		
2.☐☐☐☐		
3.☐☐☐☐		
4.☐☐☐☐		
Total		

Rounding to Thousands

Line Up

Here are four number lines.

A _____
0   500

B _____
501   1,000

C _____
1,001   5,000

D _____
5,001   10,000

Line **C** has the numbers 1,001 through 5,000.

Which line has the point for the number?

1. ____ 1,865   **2.** ____ 943   **3.** ____ 5,350

4. ____ 499   **5.** ____ 1,721   **6.** ____ 999

7. ____ 325 + 96   **8.** ____ 807 + 284   **9.** ____ 3,581 + 1,421

10. ____ 426 + 490   **11.** ____ 75 + 179   **12.** ____ 4,843 + 78

13. ____ 2,009 + 2,901 **14.** ____ 497 + 4   **15.** ____ 352 + 4,698

Four In A Line

Here's a game for you and friend.

Rules

- Take turns.
- Pick two numbers from the sign.
- Add the numbers.
- Mark the answer on the game board. Use your **X** or **O**.

The first player with four **X**s or **O**s in a row, column, or diagonal is the winner.

X _____
Player's Name

O _____
Player's Name

47	532
789	111
428	653

GAMEBOARD

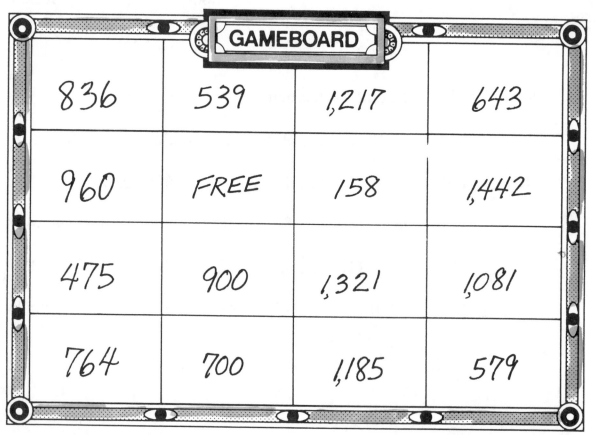

836	539	1,217	643
960	FREE	158	1,442
475	900	1,321	1,081
764	700	1,185	579

Adding 2- to 4-Digit Numbers

Subtracto

Along each line, subtract the smaller number from the larger number.

Use the work space to write the subtraction example.

Write the difference in the circle between the two numbers.

Fill in all of the circles.

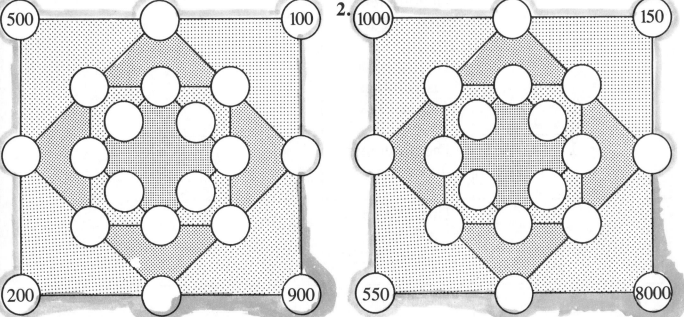

2.

Work space:

Difference Delight

Find someone to play this game with you.

Set a time limit: 2 minutes for each rule.

Each player should:

- Write subtraction examples that fit the rules.
- Subtract.
- Check the examples with the other player.
- Score 1 point for each example that fits the rule.

Player 1	Rule	Player 2
	The difference has 2 digits.	
	The difference is between 500 and 600.	
	The difference has 4 digits.	
	The difference is between 5,000 and 5,050.	
	The difference is 398.	

Total Score_____   **Total Score**_____

Missing Locks

Find the key that fits the lock.

Write the key number in the space.

1.

$$\begin{array}{r} 48 \\ \times \square \\ \hline 240 \end{array}$$

2.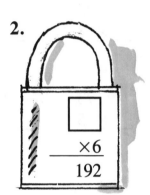

$$\begin{array}{r} \square \\ \times 6 \\ \hline 192 \end{array}$$

3.

$$\begin{array}{r} \square \\ \times 3 \\ \hline 222 \end{array}$$

4.

$$\begin{array}{r} 81 \\ \times \square \\ \hline 648 \end{array}$$

5.

$$\begin{array}{r} \square \\ \times 9 \\ \hline 585 \end{array}$$

6.

$$\begin{array}{r} 158 \\ \times \square \\ \hline 316 \end{array}$$

7.

$$\begin{array}{r} \square \\ \times 4 \\ \hline 2{,}588 \end{array}$$

8.

$$\begin{array}{r} 260 \\ \times \square \\ \hline 1{,}820 \end{array}$$

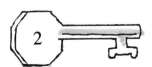 8

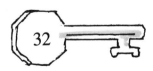 7

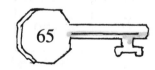 65

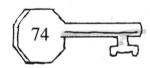 74

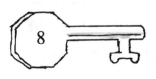 2

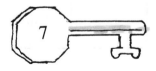 32

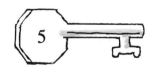 5

 647

Multiplying 2- and 3-Digit Numbers by 1-Digit Numbers

Multiplication Bingo

Ask someone at home to play this game with you.

Each player chooses a board.

Take turns picking a multiplication example and finding the product.

Both players write an **X** on the product on their boards.

The first player to get four in a row, column, or diagonal is the winner.

46	29	265	403	25	81	519	4(
× 2	× 9	× 8	× 8	× 3	× 7	× 4	×

11	578	126	314	73	289	162	2:
× 6	× 9	× 5	× 7	× 5	× 3	× 4	×

Player 1

462	365	2,442	261
2,120	3,224	66	867
75	5,202	630	567
92	648	2,076	2,198

Player 2

867	3,224	2,076	75
648	630	567	365
5,202	261	2,120	462
66	2,442	92	2,198

The Product Is The Fruit

LESSON **10**

Multiply.
Put the letters in the correct boxes to name the fruits.

1.

P									

100   200   300   400   500   600   700   800   900   1000

P 14	P 26	L 17	E 45
× 12	× 30	× 50	× 10
28			
140			
168			

N 19	E 33	I 15	P 52	A 25
× 20	× 30	× 15	× 13	× 21

2.

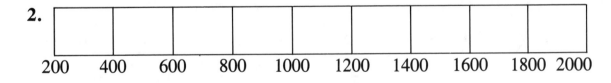

200   400   600   800   1000   1200   1400   1600   1800   2000

A 24	C 30	P 47	L 26
× 20	× 10	× 40	× 50

O 45	N 36	U 53	A 69	T 30
× 32	× 22	× 33	× 15	× 30

Get To The Other Side

This is a game for two players or teams.
One team is the **X** team.
The other team is the **O** team.

Rules:

- Take turns.

- Pick two numbers on the sign.

- Multiply.

- If the answer is on the game board,
  mark your **X** or **O** on the answer.

10	54
21	60
32	70
43	90

The winner is the first team to make a path connecting
its two sides of the game board.

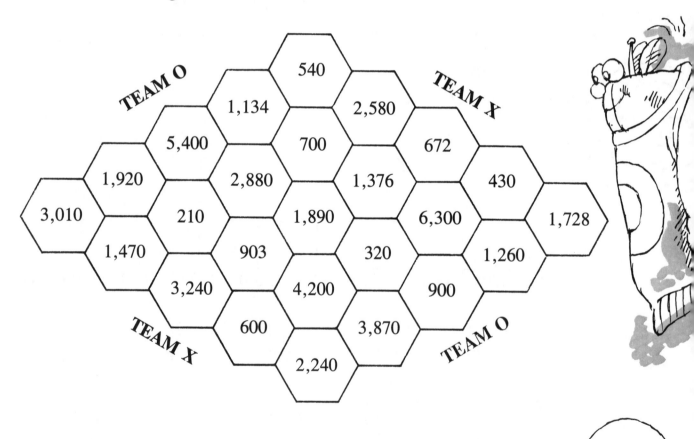

LESSON
11

Number Facts

Divide.
The answer is a number fact.

1. 9)90   The number of
           dimes equal to
           one dollar

2. 3)93   The number of
           days in
           December

3. 4)48   The number of
           eggs in a dozen

4. 2)52   The number
           of letters in
           the alphabet

5. 3)396   The number of
           rooms in the
           White House

6. 6)600   The number
           of years in
           in a century

7. 8)816   The number of
           stories in the
           Empire State
           Building

8. 5)250   The number
           of states in
           the United
           States

9. 7)280   The number of
           nickels in a
           roll of nickels

10. 2)176   The number
           of keys on
           a piano

U.S. Game

This is a game for you and your family.
First, each player tries to answer the questions.
Then divide to check your answers.
The quotient gives the answer to the question.
Ring the correct answer.
The winner is the one with the most correct answers.
There can be more than one winner.

1. 4)84‾   How many stars were on the U.S. flag made by Betsy Ross in 1777?

20	The flag had 7 stars.
21	The flag had 13 stars.
22	The flag had 48 stars.
41	The flag had 50 stars.

2. 3)54‾   How many U.S. Senators are there today?

11	There are 50 senators.
16	There are 75 senators.
18	There are 100 senators.
28	There are 150 senators.

3. 5)70‾   How many Supreme Court Justices are there?

12	There are 5 justices.
14	There are 9 justices.
22	There are 13 justices.
24	There are 15 justices.

4. 2)826‾   How old was John Hancock when he signed the Declaration of Independence?

213	Hancock was 85 years old.
403	Hancock was 72 years old.
412	Hancock was 65 years old.
413	Hancock was 39 years old.

5. 3)642‾   In what year was Washington, D.C. chosen as the capital of the United States?

210	Washington, D.C. was chosen in 1900.
211	Washington, D.C. was chosen in 1865.
213	Washington, D.C. was chosen in 1801.
214	Washington, D.C. was chosen in 1790.

   Dividing 2- and 3-Digit Numbers by 1-Digit Numbers

Estimating Quotients

LESSON
12

Pick a number from the cloud to make the sentence true.

1. 840 ÷ ☐ is between 20 and 30.

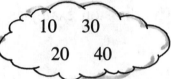

10   30
20   40

2. 960 ÷ ☐ is between 40 and 50.

20   60
40   80

3. 770 ÷ ☐ is between 10 and 20.

10   50
30   70

4. 590 ÷ ☐ is between 50 and 60.

60   10
50   30

5. 480 ÷ ☐ is between 10 and 20.

30   10
50   70

6. 680 ÷ ☐ is between 30 and 40.

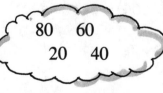

80   60
20   40

A Presidential Quiz

This is a quiz for you and your family.

Can you put the presidents in order?

Make a guess.

Write the names.

Then check by matching the number beside each name with the answers to the division examples.

The division examples tell you the order of the presidents.

Your list:

John Kennedy	27
Thomas Jefferson	8
Abraham Lincoln	7
Ronald Reagan	5
George Washington	38
Dwight Eisenhower	81
Franklin Roosevelt	3
Andrew Jackson	12

1. _____
2. _____
3. _____
4. _____
5. _____
6. _____
7. _____
8. _____

1. $19\overline{)722}$ **2.** $30\overline{)240}$ **3.** $57\overline{)684}$ **4.** $79\overline{)553}$

5. $64\overline{)192}$ **6.** $11\overline{)891}$ **7.** $23\overline{)621}$ **8.** $58\overline{)290}$

Out Of Place

In each row, one answer is different.

Ring the answer that is different.

1.

3)‾900‾

2.
     5,296
  − 4,996

3.
     175
  ×   2

4.
     293
  +   7

5.
     118
  + 323

6.
      21
  ×   21

7.
   2,064
  −   623

8.

2)‾882‾

9.
     286
  +   39

10.

3)‾972‾

11.
   8,974
  − 8,649

12.
      65
  ×   5

13.
      23
  ×   22

14.

2)‾992‾

15.
     199
  + 297

16.
   3,991
  − 3,495

High-Low

This is a game to play with a friend.

Use cards or pieces of paper to make number cards like these.

Rules:

■ Take turns.

■ Mix up the cards and turn the pile face down.

■ Pick two cards.

■ Use the cards and +, −, × or ÷ to make a
   true number sentence.

Scoring:

■ If the answer is greater than 100, score 2 points.

■ If the answer is less than 30, score 2 points.

■ If the answer is between 30 and 100, score 1 point.

The player with the greater total score after five turns is the winner.

Players:		
Turn 1		
Turn 2		
Turn 3		
Turn 4		
Turn 5		
Total Score		

Using Mixed Operations with Whole Numbers

It Takes Time

Find the start time.
Then match the person with the start time
to identify the activity.

1. Carol's activity took 30 minutes.
She stopped at 4:15.
She started at _____ .
Carol _____ .
(activity)

2. John's activity took 50 minutes.
He stopped at 5:50.
John started at _____ .
John _____ .

3. Bob's activity took 1 hour
20 minutes.
He stopped at 6:00.
Bob started at _____ .
Bob _____ .

4. Sue's activity took 2 hours
35 minutes.
She stopped at 7:45.
Sue started at _____ .
Sue _____ .

5. Ken's activity took 1 hour
5 minutes.
He stopped at 1:00.
Ken started at _____ .
Ken _____ .

6. Ann's activity took
17 minutes.
She stopped at 3:10.
Ann started at _____ .
Ann _____ .

Start Time	Activity
5:10	saw a movie
3:45	jogged to the park
2:53	biked to the store
5:00	practiced the piano
4:40	played basketball
11:55	baked bread

Time It

Ask an adult to help you with this activity.
You will need a watch or clock with a minute hand.

For each activity, record the start and stop times.
Then fill in the elapsed time.
The elapsed time is the number of minutes it takes for you to do
the activity.

Activity	Start Time	Stop Time	Elapsed Time (in minutes)
1. Eat breakfast			
2. Do homework			
3. Clean dishes after dinner			
4. Play a game			
5. Watch a television program			
6. Get ready for bed			

Which activity took the most time? _____

Which activity took the least time? _____

Using Elapsed Time

Centimeter Jumble

Get a centimeter ruler.
Measure each line segment.
Use the code to find the letter for each length.
Unscramble the letters to make a word.

The word
is LET.

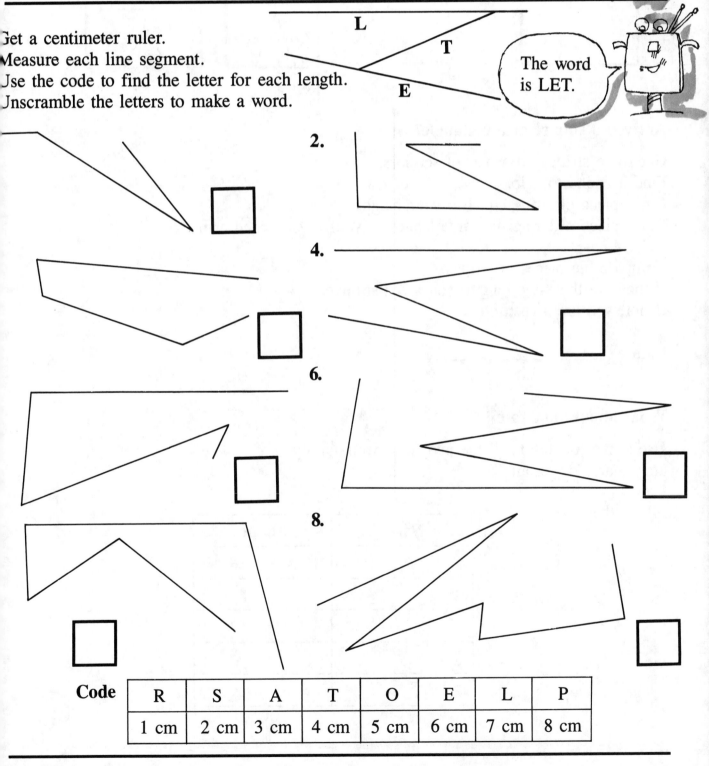

Code	R	S	A	T	O	E	L	P
	1 cm	2 cm	3 cm	4 cm	5 cm	6 cm	7 cm	8 cm

Are You Square?

Some people are **squares.**

Some people are **rectangles.**

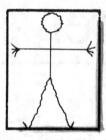 

Are you a **square** or a **rectangle?**

Get some string and a pair of scissors.
Find a friend to help.
Cut a piece of string equal to your height.
Cut a piece of string the same length as your outstretched arms.

Compare the pieces of strings.
If they are the same length, you are a **square.**
If not, you are a **rectangle.**

I am a _____.

What about your family?

Use string to find out if the people in your family
are squares or rectangles.

Fill in the table.

Name	Shape

Cross-Measures

Read the clue.
Write the unit of measure in the cross-measures puzzle.

ACROSS

2. 2 pints = 1 _____.

4. A loaf of bread weighs about 1 _____.

6. A drinking glass holds about 1 _____ of water.

8. 5,280 feet = 1 _____.

9. A postage stamp is about 1 _____ wide.

10. A sheet of paper is about 1 _____ long.

DOWN

1. 36 inches = 1 _____.

3. A small car weighs about 1 _____.

5. A letter weighs about 1 _____.

7. 2 cups = 1 _____.

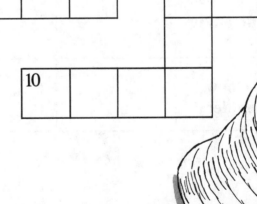

Measurement Estimation

Do this activity with a friend.
Estimate first.
Measure to the nearest inch.
Then ring the closer estimate.

Estimate the length	Your Estimate	Friend's Estimate	Measurement
around your wrist			
of your foot			
from your knee to the floor			
of your thumbnail			
around your ankle			
from your elbow to your shoulder			

Using Customary Units

Zoo Plot

Here is a drawing of the Johnson City Zoo.

Each ☐ stands for 1 square unit.

Johnson City Zoo

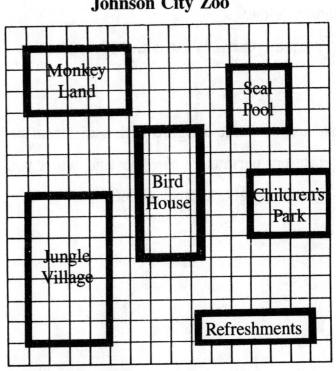

Fill in the blanks.

1. The area of Jungle Village is _____ square units.

2. The perimeter of the Seal Pool is _____ units.

3. The area of Monkey Land is _____ square units.

4. The perimeter of the Bird House is _____ units.

5. The _____ has a perimeter of 10 units.

6. The _____ has an area of 9 square units.

7. The _____ has a perimeter of 14 units.

8. The _____ and the _____ have the same area.

Finding Perimeter and Area

Geo Challenge

Here is a challenge for you and your family.

Cut out **9 squares** of paper.

Use all of the squares to make a figure.

Squares must share sides.

OK OK NOT OK NOT OK

Draw the figure below.

The area is 9 square units. What is the perimeter?

Use the 9 squares to make a figure with a different perimeter.

How many different perimeters can you find when you use the 9 squares? _____

Draw each figure and give the perimeter.

Finding Perimeter and Area

Building Sense

Each  costs $1.

What is the cost of each of these buildings?

1.

2.

3.

4.

5.

6.

Riddle Riot

This is a riddle for you and your family.

Take turns. Multiply to find the volume of each figure.

Write the letter of the figure on the line above the volume of that figure.

HOW ARE COFFEE AND DIRT ALIKE?

R

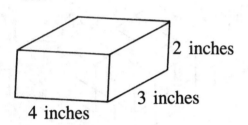

2 inches
3 inches
4 inches

Volume = _____ cubic inches

U

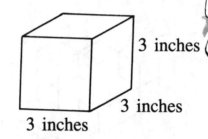

3 inches
3 inches
3 inches

Volume = _____ cubic inches

O

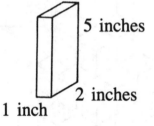

5 inches
2 inches
1 inch

Volume = _____ cubic inches

D

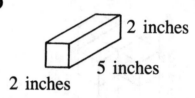

2 inches
5 inches
2 inches

Volume = _____ cubic inches

N

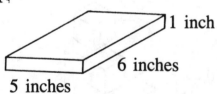

1 inch
6 inches
5 inches

Volume = _____ cubic inches

G

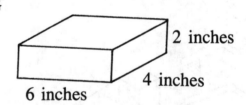

2 inches
4 inches
6 inches

Volume = _____ cubic inches

THEY BOTH ARE ___ ___ ___ ___ ___ ___ .
48   24   10   27   30   20

Multiplying to Find Volume

Geography Quiz

LESSON
20

First try to answer the question.
Then ring the fraction that is not equivalent to other fractions.
That fraction gives the answer.

1. Which state does not have an ocean coastline?

$\frac{1}{4}$ Oregon $\frac{3}{8}$ Kansas $\frac{12}{16}$ Washington $\frac{2}{8}$ South Carolina

2. Which state was not one of the 13 original states?

$\frac{4}{40}$ Rhode Island $\frac{1}{10}$ Pennsylvania $\frac{3}{20}$ Ohio $\frac{6}{60}$ Virginia

3. Which state does not border Canada?

$\frac{4}{6}$ Montana $\frac{4}{5}$ Colorado $\frac{10}{15}$ North Dakota $\frac{2}{3}$ Maine

4. Which state's capital does not begin with B?

$\frac{2}{11}$ Nebraska $\frac{5}{30}$ Idaho $\frac{3}{18}$ Massachusetts $\frac{1}{6}$ Louisiana

5. Which state does not border Mexico?

$\frac{18}{30}$ California $\frac{3}{5}$ Texas $\frac{12}{20}$ Arizona $\frac{24}{42}$ Mississippi

6. Which state does not border one of the Great Lakes?

$\frac{1}{4}$ Iowa $\frac{15}{40}$ Michigan $\frac{24}{64}$ New York $\frac{3}{8}$ Minnesota

---

Using Equivalent Fractions

Odd One Out

This is an activity for you and a friend. Take turns.
One fraction in each row is not equivalent to the others.
Ring the fraction that is not equivalent.
Write its letter above the row number on the bottom of the page.
The letters will spell the name of a famous comic book character.

1.	**A** $\frac{6}{12}$	**B** $\frac{5}{10}$	**S** $\frac{4}{7}$	**R** $\frac{1}{2}$
2.	**T** $\frac{2}{6}$	**U** $\frac{3}{6}$	**O** $\frac{1}{3}$	**X** $\frac{3}{9}$
3.	**J** $\frac{1}{4}$	**V** $\frac{3}{12}$	**C** $\frac{2}{8}$	**P** $\frac{4}{10}$
4.	**E** $\frac{5}{15}$	**Z** $\frac{1}{5}$	**F** $\frac{3}{15}$	**W** $\frac{4}{20}$
5.	**D** $\frac{2}{3}$	**R** $\frac{4}{9}$	**Y** $\frac{4}{6}$	**I** $\frac{8}{12}$
6.	**Z** $\frac{1}{6}$	**L** $\frac{3}{18}$	**M** $\frac{6}{12}$	**Q** $\frac{2}{12}$
7.	**K** $\frac{6}{8}$	**G** $\frac{3}{4}$	**S** $\frac{12}{16}$	**A** $\frac{3}{8}$
8.	**N** $\frac{6}{8}$	**Q** $\frac{6}{10}$	**H** $\frac{3}{5}$	**T** $\frac{9}{15}$

$\overline{}$ $\quad$ $\overline{}$ $\quad$ $\overline{}$ $\quad$ $\overline{}$ $\quad$ $\overline{}$ $\quad$ $\overline{}$ $\quad$ $\overline{}$ $\quad$ $\overline{}$

1 $\qquad$ 2 $\qquad$ 3 $\qquad$ 4 $\qquad$ 5 $\qquad$ 6 $\qquad$ 7 $\qquad$ 8

Using Equivalent Fractions

Mystery Answer

Write the mixed number or whole number for each fraction.
Cross off the number on the chart.
The number that is left is the answer to the question.

$2\frac{1}{3}$	$1\frac{2}{5}$	2	$1\frac{3}{10}$
3	$5\frac{1}{3}$	$2\frac{3}{4}$	$1\frac{1}{8}$
$2\frac{1}{6}$	$1\frac{5}{8}$	4	5
6	$2\frac{1}{2}$	$1\frac{1}{10}$	$2\frac{5}{6}$

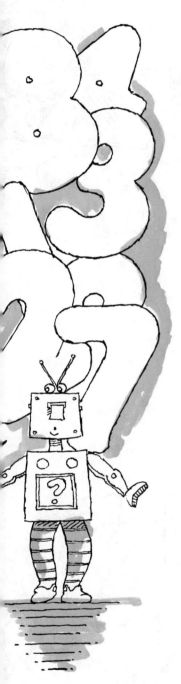

HOW MANY PIPES ARE ON A BAGPIPE?

1. $\frac{5}{2} =$ **2.** $\frac{7}{3} =$ **3.** $\frac{11}{4} =$ **4.** $\frac{13}{10} =$

5. $\frac{8}{4} =$ **6.** $\frac{13}{6} =$ **7.** $\frac{7}{5} =$ **8.** $\frac{16}{3} =$

9. $\frac{24}{4} =$ **10.** $\frac{8}{2} =$ **11.** $\frac{15}{5} =$ **12.** $\frac{9}{8} =$

13. $\frac{11}{10} =$ **14.** $\frac{17}{6} =$ **15.** $\frac{13}{8} =$

THERE ARE _____ PIPES ON A BAGPIPE.

Nicknames

This is a matching game for you and a friend.

- You will each need a piece of paper.
- Make a list of the 10 states. Write the nickname for each state.
- Then draw a line to match each fraction with its mixed number or whole number. The matching number gives the nickname for the state.
- Score 1 point for each correct match on your list.
- The player with the greater score is the winner.

State		Nickname	
1. Alaska	$\frac{8}{3}$	$1\frac{1}{2}$	Grand Canyon State
2. Arizona	$\frac{3}{2}$	$3\frac{1}{3}$	Magnolia State
3. California	$\frac{9}{4}$	$2\frac{2}{3}$	Land of the Midnight Sun
4. Florida	$\frac{7}{6}$	$1\frac{1}{6}$	Sunshine State
5. Georgia	$\frac{16}{4}$	5	Treasure State
6. Kentucky	$\frac{18}{5}$	$2\frac{1}{4}$	Golden State
7. Mississippi	$\frac{10}{3}$	$8\frac{1}{2}$	Beehive State
8. Montana	$\frac{15}{3}$	4	Peach State
9. New Jersey	$\frac{11}{6}$	$3\frac{3}{5}$	Bluegrass State
10. Utah	$\frac{17}{2}$	$1\frac{5}{6}$	Garden State

Finding Mixed Numbers

Fraction Action

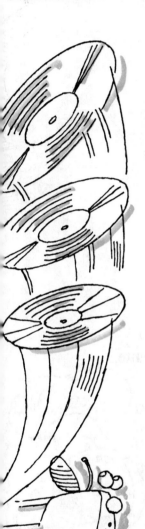

Who Invented The Phonograph?

Guess first.
Add or subtract.
Write the answer in lowest terms.
Then write the letter of the problem on the line above the answer.

D. $\dfrac{2}{5}$ $+\dfrac{1}{5}$

H. $\dfrac{3}{7}$ $+\dfrac{3}{7}$

A. $\dfrac{6}{6}$ $-\dfrac{1}{6}$

I. $\dfrac{2}{3}$ $-\dfrac{1}{3}$

O. $\dfrac{4}{10}$ $+\dfrac{5}{10}$

S. $\dfrac{8}{9}$ $-\dfrac{1}{9}$

M. $\dfrac{3}{5}$ $-\dfrac{1}{5}$

E. $\dfrac{1}{8}$ $+\dfrac{5}{8}$

N. $\dfrac{5}{6}$ $-\dfrac{1}{6}$

O. $\dfrac{7}{10}$ $+\dfrac{1}{10}$

S. $\dfrac{1}{8}$ $+\dfrac{1}{8}$

T. $\dfrac{7}{12}$ $-\dfrac{1}{12}$

$\dfrac{1}{2}$ $\dfrac{6}{7}$ $\dfrac{9}{10}$ $\dfrac{2}{5}$ $\dfrac{5}{6}$ $\dfrac{1}{4}$ $\dfrac{3}{4}$ $\dfrac{3}{5}$ $\dfrac{1}{3}$ $\dfrac{7}{9}$ $\dfrac{4}{5}$ $\dfrac{2}{3}$

Recipe Matters

Have someone in your family help you with this activity.
Complete the recipe to make 12 muffins.

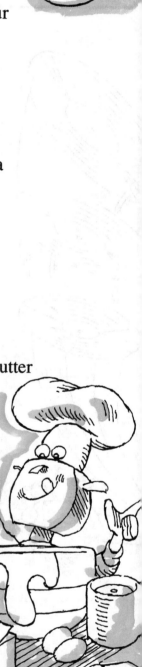

Bran Muffins - Makes 6	Bran Muffins - Makes 12
$\frac{1}{2}$ cup whole grain flour	_____ cup whole grain flour
$\frac{1}{8}$ teaspoon salt	_____ teaspoon salt
$\frac{3}{8}$ cup of bran	_____ cup of bran
$\frac{1}{4}$ teaspoon baking soda	_____ teaspoon baking soda
$\frac{1}{2}$ cup buttermilk	_____ cup buttermilk
1 beaten egg	_____ beaten eggs
$\frac{1}{8}$ cup molasses	_____ cup molasses
1 tablespoon melted butter	_____ tablespoons melted butter

If you have the ingredients, you might like to work with an adult
to make the bran muffins.

- Preheat the oven to 350° Fahrenheit.
- Mix the flour, bran, salt, and baking soda in a bowl.
- Beat the buttermilk, eggs, molasses, and butter in another bowl.
- Add the dry mixture to the liquid mixture. Mix.
- Pour the mixture into a muffin pan.
- Bake for 25 minutes.

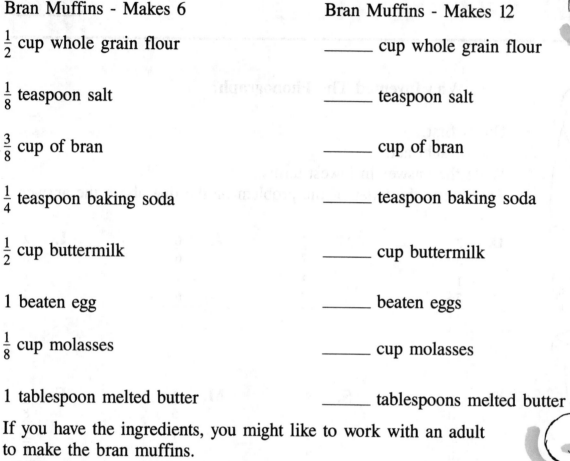

Decimal Number Logic

Use the clues to form the numbers.

1. Use: 2, 3, 4, 6

Clues:
- The 3 is in the tenths place.
- The number in the hundreds place is half the number in the tens place.
- The number in the ones place is the sum of the numbers in the hundreds place and the tens place.

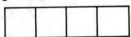

3. Use: 3, 5, 8, 9

Clues:
- The greatest number is in the hundredths place.
- The number in the tenths place is 2 less than the number in the tens place.

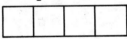

5. Use: 0, 5, 6, 7, 9

Clues:
- The number in the hundredths place is 9 more than the number in the tenths place.
- The 6 is in the tens place.
- The number in the hundreds place is greater than the number in the ones place.

2. Use: 0, 1, 2, 5

Clues:
- The number in the tens place is 5 less than the number in the hundreds place.
- The number in the tenths place is twice the number in the ones place.

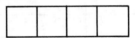

4. Use: 4, 8, 7, 7

Clues:
- The numbers in the tens place and the tenths place are the same.
- The greatest number is in the hundredths place.

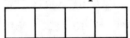

6. Use: 2, 4, 6, 7, 8

Clues:
- The number in the hundredths place is twice the number in the tenths place.
- The 7 is in the ones place.
- The number in the hundreds place is three times the number in the tens place.

Decimal Toss

Play this game with a friend.

Rules

- Take turns.
- Toss a coin onto the playing board.
- Score the number on which the coin lands.
- After five rounds, the player with the greater number of points is the winner.

5.8 = 5.80
5.80 scores
10 points

Scoring

5 points if the digit in the hundredths place is 5 or less
5 points if the digit in the tenths place is 5 or more

6.23	17.4	8.43	0.51
31.6	5.72	3.54	0.12
28.8	0.02	40.1	15.27
52.6	7.49	0.58	2.96

	Player _____	Player _____
Round 1		
Round 2		
Round 3		
Round 4		
Round 5		
Total		

Field Day

The Palmer Elementary School held a field day. Write each student's name next to the correct finishing time.

1.
I finished last.

Richard

2.
I finished first.

Julio

3.
I finished just before Richard.

Lisa

4.
I finished just after Julio.

Maria

Race Results	
Name	Time (in seconds)
	13.05
	12.45
	12.56
	13.0
	14.3
	14.25

5.
I finished before Kim.

Tony

6
I finished just after Tony.

Kim

Decimal Tournament

2, 3, or 4 people can play this game.

You need 1 number cube.

Take turns.

On each turn:

- Roll the number cube.
- Write the number in a box.

After each player has had four turns, read the numbers.

The player with the greatest number wins.

Player 1 ☐ ☐ • ☐ ☐

Player 2 ☐ ☐ • ☐ ☐

Player 3 ☐ ☐ • ☐ ☐

Player 4 ☐ ☐ • ☐ ☐

What was the winning number? _____

Park It Right

IN WHAT YEAR DID THE FIRST PARKING METER APPEAR ON A CITY STREET?

THE YEAR WAS _____ _____ _____ _____ .

1.

$$6.42 + 5.93$$ $$7.12 - 0.82$$

The only digit that is in both answers is _____.

Write this digit in the tens place of the year.

2.

$$8.56 + 3.8$$ $$9.04 - 3.9$$

The only digit that is in both answers is _____.

Write this digit in the thousands place of the year.

3.

$$12.7 + 2.73$$ $$1.26 - 0.7$$

The only digit that is in both answers is _____.

Write this digit in the ones place of the year.

4.

$$18.95 + 39.96$$ $$24.01 - 3.22$$

The only digit that is in both answers is _____.

Write this digit in the hundreds place of the year.

Adding and Subtracting with Decimals

Choose It Right

Play this game with a friend.

- Take turns.
- Pick two numbers from the chart.
- Add or subtract the numbers.
- Score your answer.
- Cross off the numbers on the chart.

12.31	4.37	61.3	0.52
3.8	42.7	15.6	19.3
6.94	1.8	5.09	29.6
25.28	0.65	48.2	35.66
0.07	29.9	0.76	8.29

After five rounds, the player with the greater total score is the winner.

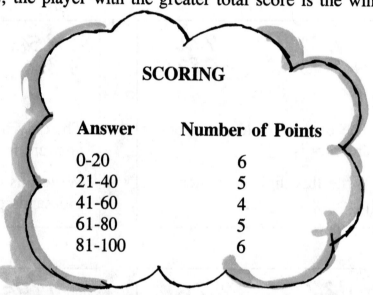

SCORING

Answer	Number of Points
0-20	6
21-40	5
41-60	4
61-80	5
81-100	6

	Player _____	Player _____
Round 1		
Round 2		
Round 3		
Round 4		
Round 5		
Total		

Adding and Subtracting with Decimals

Which Way To Go?

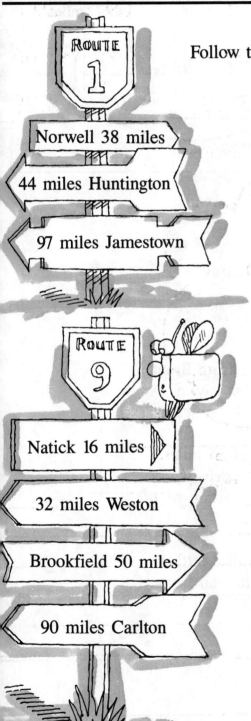

Follow the signs and stay on the Routes to complete these facts.

1. You are traveling on Route 1. It is _____ miles from Jamestown to Huntington.

2. You are traveling on Route 1. It is _____ miles from Jamestown to Norwell.

3. You leave Jamestown for Huntington. When you are 30 miles from Jamestown, you are _____ miles from Huntington.

4. You leave Norwell for Jamestown. When you are 60 miles from Norwell, you are _____ miles from Jamestown.

5. You are traveling on Route 9. It is _____ miles from Weston to Carlton.

6. You are traveling on Route 9. At 45 miles per hour, it would take _____ hours to drive from the sign to Carlton.

7. You are traveling on Route 9. It is _____ miles from Natick to Brookfield and back to Natick.

8. You leave Carlton for Brookfield. When you are 100 miles from Brookfield, you are _____ miles from Carlton.

Mystery Map

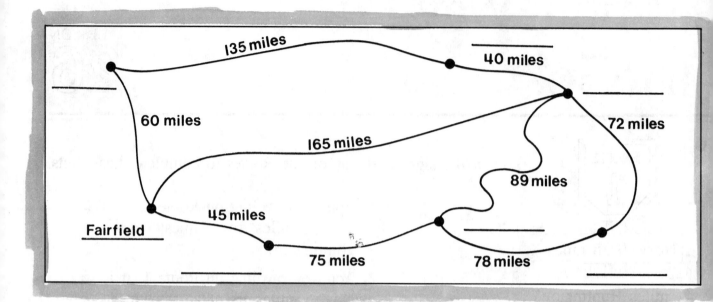

135 miles

40 miles

60 miles

72 miles

165 miles

89 miles

Fairfield

45 miles

75 miles

78 miles

Work with a friend.
Take turns reading the clues.
Use the clues to name the cities.
Write the names of the cities on the lines on the map.

CLUES

1. The distance from Fairfield to Brent is 60 miles.

2. The distance from Brent to Danvers by way of Fairfield is 105 miles.

3. The distance from Brent to Edgetown is three times the distance from Danvers to Fairfield.

4. At a speed of 55 miles per hour, the drive from Fairfield to Carlton would take 3 hours.

5. The roundtrip distance from Carlton to Granite is 144 miles.

6. Alton is 3 miles farther from Granite than from Danvers.

Using Information on a Map

Jogging Time

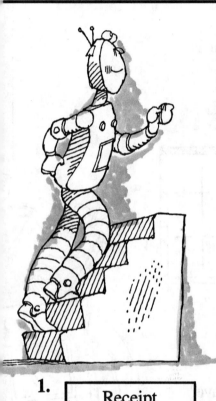

SALE!

$22.00

$5.50

$9.00

$12.50

$2.50

Fill in the receipts below with items from the sale sign.
The sum of the costs must equal the total shown.
No one bought more than one of each item.

1.

Receipt
sweatshirt $12.50
_____
_____
TOTAL: $15.00

2.

Receipt
_____
_____
TOTAL: $18.00

3.

Receipt
_____
_____
TOTAL: $14.50

Receipt
_____
_____
TOTAL: $43.50

5.

Receipt
_____
_____
TOTAL: $30.00

6.

Receipt
_____
_____
_____
TOTAL: $33.50

Tic-Tac-Toe

Ask someone to play this game with you.
Each player should use the nine numbers in the box
to fill in a Tic-Tac-Toe board.
Take turns choosing a problem below.
Solve it together.
Find the answer on the Tic-Tac-Toe boards.
Mark an **X** on the answer.
The first player to get three **X**s in a row, column, or diagonal is
the winner.

Player 1

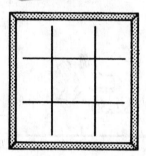

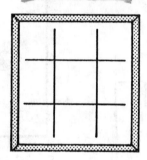

12   4
1
33
5
0   9
3
7

Player 2

I have 16¢.
I have 3 coins.
How many pennies do I have?

I have 45¢.
I have 5 coins.
I do not have a dime.
How many nickels do I have?

What number can you add to
10 or subtract from 20 and
get the same answer?

I am 6 years older than my
sister. The sum of our ages is
12. How old am I?

We lost the game by 2 runs.
A total of 8 runs were scored
in all. How many runs did
we score?

Add me to 75 and you get 92.
What do you get when you
subtract me from 50?

I am thinking of two numbers.
Their sum is 8.
Their product is 16.
What is their difference?

If you divide the mystery
number by 2 and then add 1,
you get 7.
What is the mystery number?

Guessing and Checking

What's The Number?

Use the clues to find the answer.
Make lists to help you.

Work Space

1. ■ The number is greater than 25.
   ■ The number is less than 35.
   ■ You say the number when you count by 3s.
   ■ You say the number when you count by 10s.
   ■ The number is _____.

2. ■ The number is between 40 and 60.
   ■ It is an even number.
   ■ The sum of the digits is 7.
   ■ The number is _____.

3. ■ The number is a multiple of 5.
   ■ It is less than 25.
   ■ It is a two-digit number.
   ■ It is not a multiple of 10.
   ■ The number is _____.

4. ■ The number is between 242 and 250.
   ■ Each digit is even.
   ■ Two of the digits are the same.
   ■ The number is _____.

5. ■ The number is between 300 and 340.
   ■ The sum of the digits is 6.
   ■ When you divide by 5, the remainder is 0.
   ■ The number is _____.

Tic-Tac-Score

This is a game for you and a friend.
Each player tries to get the greatest number of **X**s or **O**s in
the same row (horizontally, vertically, or diagonally).

Take turns writing an **X** or an **O** in the squares.
When the board has been filled in, find the score.

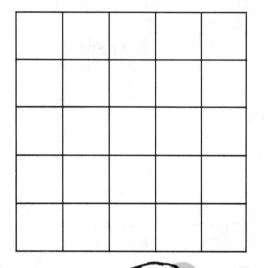

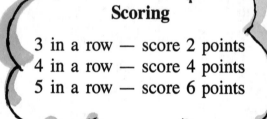

Scoring

3 in a row — score 2 points
4 in a row — score 4 points
5 in a row — score 6 points

Player 1

has _____ 3 in a row for _____ points.

has _____ 4 in a row for _____ points.

has _____ 5 in a row for _____ points.

TOTAL SCORE: _____

Player 2

has _____ 3 in a row for _____ points.

has _____ 4 in a row for _____ points.

has _____ 5 in a row for _____ points.

TOTAL SCORE: _____

The winner is _____.

Using Thinking Skills

Place The Facts

Use the numbers on the signs to fill in the blanks.
Make sure that the numbers you choose make sense.

10

300   50

1. The Green family went on a trip. On the first day, they traveled
about _____ miles in 6 hours. That is an average of _____
miles each hour. Their car used _____ gallons of gasoline.

22.75
8.50
2.50
3.25

2. On the first night, the Greens went out for dinner. They
ordered two pizzas. Each pizza cost $_____. They also
ordered a large salad that cost $_____ and a pitcher of juice
for $_____. The juice cost more than the salad. Altogether,
they spent $_____.

3   20
5
1

3. On the second day, the Greens went to an amusement park.
They bought two adult tickets for $_____ each and three
children's tickets for $_____ each. The total cost of the tickets
was $19. They got $_____ change from $_____.

3.60   1.80

0.90   2.75

4. On the third day, the Greens stopped at a supermarket to buy
supplies for a picnic. Eric bought a jar of jelly for $_____.
Ann bought a jar of peanut butter. The peanut butter cost twice
as much as the jelly or $_____. Lisa bought bread for
$_____. The bread cost half as much as the jelly. Mrs. Green
bought paper plates and napkins for $_____.

Food Facts

This is an activity for you and your family to do together.

We looked at some boxes and cans and wrote down some food facts.

Then we made up some problems.

Work together to solve our problems.

Use the numbers on the products to fill in the blanks. The numbers must make sense.

1. The box of cereal weighs 360 grams. There are 12 servings per box. Each serving weighs _____ grams. There are _____ calories in each serving. With skim milk, there are 40 more calories in each serving or a total of _____ calories in each serving.

2. The can of tuna serves 3 people. The total weight of the contents of the can is _____ grams. Each serving weighs _____ grams. Each serving has 60 calories and contains 14 grams of protein. Eating all of the tuna in the can provides a person with _____ calories and _____ grams of protein.

Now that you have the idea, look for a box or a can of food and make up a problem of your own. Write your problem here. Make sure that the numbers make sense. If you need more space, use another sheet of paper.

What's The Problem?

Write two problems for each advertisement.
Then use the facts in the advertisement to solve the problems.

3 pounds
bananas
99¢

Dan wrote:

What is the cost of one pound
of bananas?

$$3)\overline{99}$$ = 33

One pound of bananas costs
33¢.

Lisa wrote:

I bought 6 pounds of bananas.
How much money did I
spend?

$$\begin{array}{r} \$0.99 \\ + \ .99 \\ \hline \$1.98 \end{array}$$

I spent $1.98.

1.
Potatoes
5 pounds
for
70¢

2.
Crick Crackle Cereal
Regular Price $1.75
Sale Price $1.49

3.
Car Rental
Jeep $15 a day
Van $17 a day

4.
Help
Wanted
Rake Leaves
$4 an hour
Cut Grass
$5 an hour

Problem Machines

Ask a friend to do this activity with you.

1. Cut out an advertisement from a newspaper or a magazine.

2. Paste the advertisement on this piece of paper.

3. Both you and your friend write problems for the advertisement. Then use the facts in the advertisement to solve the problems.

4. Read each other's problems.

TALK ABOUT THE PROBLEMS.

- Which problem do you both like the best? Why?
- Which problem was the easiest to solve?
- Which problem was the most difficult to solve?

Science Museum Trip

Write a word from the Word Box in each blank.
Then answer the questions.

WORD BOX

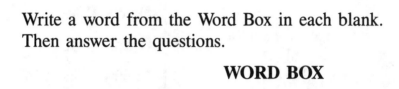

amazing	electricity	magnets	planets
beautiful	galaxies	Martians	porcupines
big	games	mushy	songs
dinosaur	gorilla	noodles	table
dragons	haunted	old	yellow

1. The fourth grade students went on a field trip to the Science Museum. They rode to the museum in 4 _____ buses. Four adults and 55 students rode on each bus. They sang _____ and played _____. How many people went to the museum in all?

_____

2. In the Space Room, Wanda liked the moon rocks best. She thought they were _____ and _____. There were 4 cases with 25 moon rocks in each case and 2 more moon rocks on the _____. How many moon rocks were there in all?

_____

3. Eric went to the Star Show that started at 1:15. He learned about _____ and _____. The show was 35 minutes long. Ten minutes after the show was over the Animal Show began. The Animal Show was about _____. What time did the Animal Show start?

_____

4. Mark bought a book about _____ for $4.95 at the Museum Store. He also bought a picture of a _____ for $2.50. He gave the clerk $10. What was Mark's change?

_____

At The Amusement Park

Here are some problems for you and your family to solve.

Take turns deciding the price of each ride. Each ride must cost less than $1.00. The Giant Slide must cost the most. Write the prices on the sign.

RIDES	
Ferris Wheel	_____
Giant Slide	_____
Merry Flip	_____
Octopus	_____
Sandpiper	_____

1. How much does it cost to buy 5 tickets for the Sandpiper and 1 ticket for the Ferris Wheel?

_____

2. You buy a ticket for the Merry Flip and the Octopus. What is your change from a five-dollar bill?

_____

3. What is the greatest number of tickets you can buy with $1.75?

_____

4. You buy 1 ticket for each ride. What is the total cost?

_____

5. How much more does it cost to buy 3 tickets for the Giant Slide than 3 tickets for the Sandpiper?

_____

6. Imagine that you have $3.00 to buy tickets. List the tickets you would buy and give the total cost.

_____

More. . .
Decimal Tournament

2, 3, or 4 people can play this game.

You need 1 number cube.

Take turns.

On each turn:

- Roll the number cube.

- Write the number in a box.

After each player has had four turns, read the numbers.

The player with the greatest number wins.

Player 1 ☐☐.☐☐

Player 2 ☐☐.☐☐

Player 3 ☐☐.☐☐

Player 4 ☐☐.☐☐

What was the winning number? _____

Enrichment
Reading Grade 3

AMERICAN
EDUCATION
PUBLISHING

1 Hidden Crickets

A fact about crickets is hiding in this puzzle.

i	e	a		c	o	r	i	a	e
c	e	a	k	a	e	e	t		h
o	e	a	i	r	s		a	w	i
i	e	i	t	h		i	a	t	o
e	s		e	l	e	e	g	s	

Write the missing letters in the twelve words below.
Do the words in order.
Color the boxes in the puzzle that have the letters you wrote.
Follow the same order you used to write the letters.
You will skip over many letters in the puzzle.

1. k ___ t ___

2. b ___ ___ t

3. p ___ n

4. l ___ ___ f

5. c ___ n ___

6. p ___ t

7. r ___ p

8. n ___ ___ l

9. t ___ ___

10. h ___ t

11. r ___ s ___

12. b ___ ___ t

Now write the letters you did not color in order.

___ ___ ___ ___ ___ ___ ___   ___ ___ ___ ___ ___ ___

___ ___ ___ ___ ___ ___ ___   ___ ___ ___ ___ ___.

Word Road

Play this game with an adult or a friend.
Get a small marker for each player.
A paper clip and a button will do.
Put both markers on GO.
Take turns. Toss two pennies onto a table or the floor.
If they land with two heads up, move 3 spaces on the Word Road.
If they land with two tails up, move 2 spaces.
If they land with one tail and one head up, move 1 space.
Read the word you land on.
If you land on a word with a long vowel, stay in that space.
If you land on a word with a short vowel, go back 2 spaces.
The first player to get HOME wins the game.

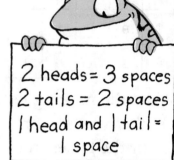

2 heads = 3 spaces
2 tails = 2 spaces
1 head and 1 tail =
1 space

Word Road

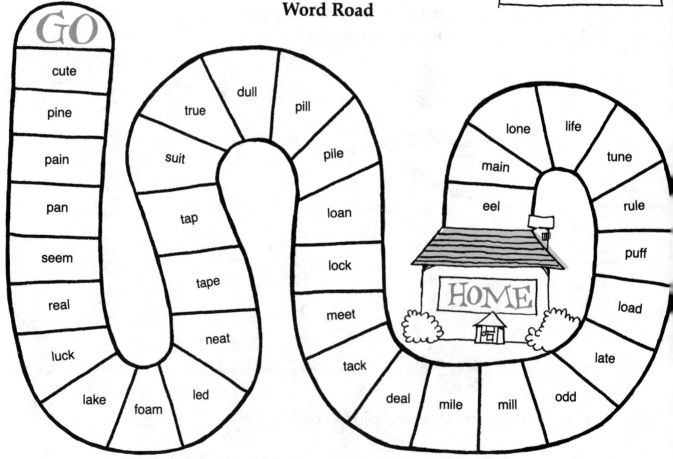

Who won? _____

2 ▸ Points for Words

Here are four word wheels.

Four word parts are on each wheel.

Add one or more letters to finish each word.

Score 5 points for every word you make.

Write your score on a piece of paper after you finish each wheel.

Try to get at least 60 points.

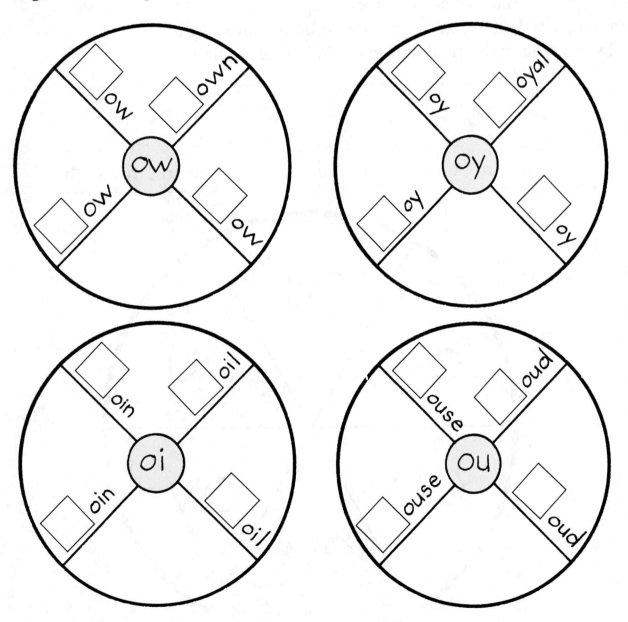

How many points did you get? _____

Break the Bank

Play this game with a friend.

Take turns.

Toss something small onto the playing board.

Look at the word part where your marker landed.

Try to make a word by adding one or more letters
from your letter bank to the word part.

You may also use other letters.

Write your word on a sheet of paper.

Cross out any letters you use from your Letter Bank.

You win if you cross out all the letters in your bank first.

My Letter Bank
f l l d b p
t c n n t h

My Friend's Letter Bank
f l l d b p
t c n n t h

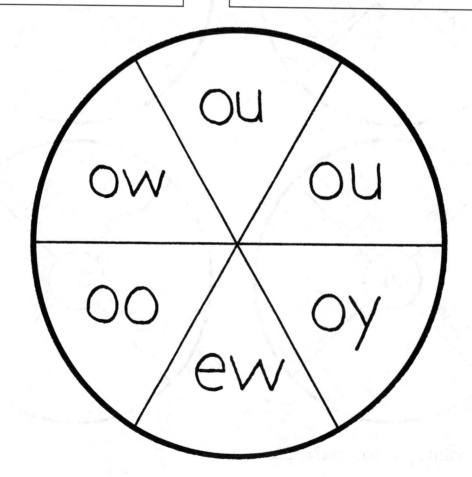

3 ⟩ Word Explosion

There has been a word explosion.
Ten words have been blown apart.
Help the frog and owl put the words back together.
Connect all the words you can.
One has been done for you.

I found silk!

si

lk

dr

ee

mp

ip

lk

sw

fr

si

la

sw

isp

nt

eam

ing

pai

ust

dr

eet

cr

cr

Forming words with consonant blends and digraphs **143**

Make a Word

Play this game with an adult.
Make number cards like these.

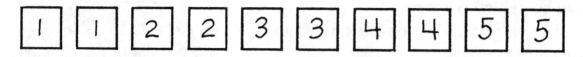

Mix up the cards and turn them face down.
Turn over one card.
The number on the card tells you which beginning letters to use.
Turn over another card.
The number on the card tells you which middle letter to use.
Turn over a third card.
The number on the card tells you which ending letters to use.
If you can use the beginning, middle, and ending letters
to make a real word, write the word on your Word Card.
Turn your cards face down after you use them.
Mix up all the cards again.
Take turns.
The first player to make three words wins the game.

Beginning	Middle	Ending
1. st	1. a	1. ck
2. cr	2. e	2. nd
3. bl	3. i	3. st
4. ch	4. o	4. mp
5. cl	5. u	5. sh

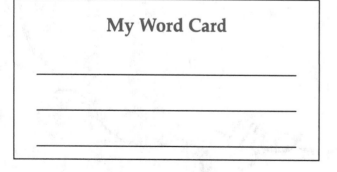

My Word Card	My Adult's Word Card
_____	_____
_____	_____
	_____

4 ▸ Odd Names

Tom Henderson decided to mix up his name.
First he wrote down all the word parts, or **syllables**, in his name.

tom   hen   der   son

Then he mixed up the syllables.

hen   son   tom   der

Finally he blended the syllables together into one word.

Hensontomder

What an odd name!

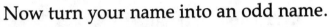

Now turn your name into an odd name.
Write your name here.

_____

Write all the syllables here.

_____

Mix up the syllables.

_____

Put them together into an odd name.

_____

Use the name of a friend to make another odd name.
Write the name here.

_____

Write all the syllables here.

_____

Mix up the syllables.

_____

Put them together into an odd name.

_____

On another sheet of paper, make up three more odd names.

The Great Mix-up

Try to turn mixed-up words into real words.
Give this page to an adult.
Have your adult read one of the mixed-up words to you.
Listen carefully.
Then try to switch the syllables until you can say a real word.
If you can say a real word, the adult colors a star for you.
Then go on to a new word.

tersis ?

1. tersis   (sister)

2. bowrain   (rainbow)

3. mintperpep   (peppermint)

4. scrapersky   (skyscraper)

5. antgi   (giant)

6. akeetpar   (parakeet)

7. derspi   (spider)

8. gerti   (tiger)

9. tapoto   (potato)

10. shotsling   (slingshot)

11. hopgrassper   (grasshopper)

12. ballfoot   (football)

13. appineple   (pineapple)

14. cubercum   (cucumber)

How many colored stars did you earn? _____

5 ▷ Bee Facts

How much do you know about bees?
Read each question.
To find the right answer, circle the correct plural
for the word in dark print.
The right answer is above the correct plural.

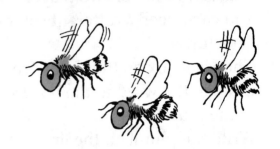

1. About how many flowers does it take to make a pound of honey?

	2,000	20,000	2,000,000
chair	chairys	chaires	chairs

2. What makes a bee's buzzing sound?

	its mouth	its wings	its legs
peach	peachs	peaches	peachess

3. Which is the only kind of bee that dies after it stings?

	a bumblebee	a killer bee	a honeybee
leaf	leafs	leafes	leaves

4. How many eggs does a queen honeybee lay in a day?

	1,500	100	15
berry	berries	berrys	berryes

5. Where does a honeybee turn nectar into honey?

	in its mouth	in its honey stomach	in small bags under its mouth
body	bodys	bodies	bodyes

Circle the number that tells how many of the bee
facts surprised you.   1   2   3   4   5

Determining correct plural forms of words   147

Color Three

This is a game for two players.
You each need a different color crayon.
Take turns.
Choose a box on the Color Three Board.
Change the word in the box from the singular
to the plural.
Write the plural on the line.
If both players agree the plural is correct, color the box.
The first player to color three boxes in a row is the winner.
The row may go up and down, across, or on a slant.

Color Three Board

shelf _____	daisy _____	slice _____
elbow _____	ash _____	child _____
bakery _____	task _____	speech _____

6 ▶ Star Lines

You can make a very big star.
Find three forms of the same word around the circle.
Use a ruler to draw straight lines to connect the words.
Keep on connecting words until the star is finished.
Then color the star.

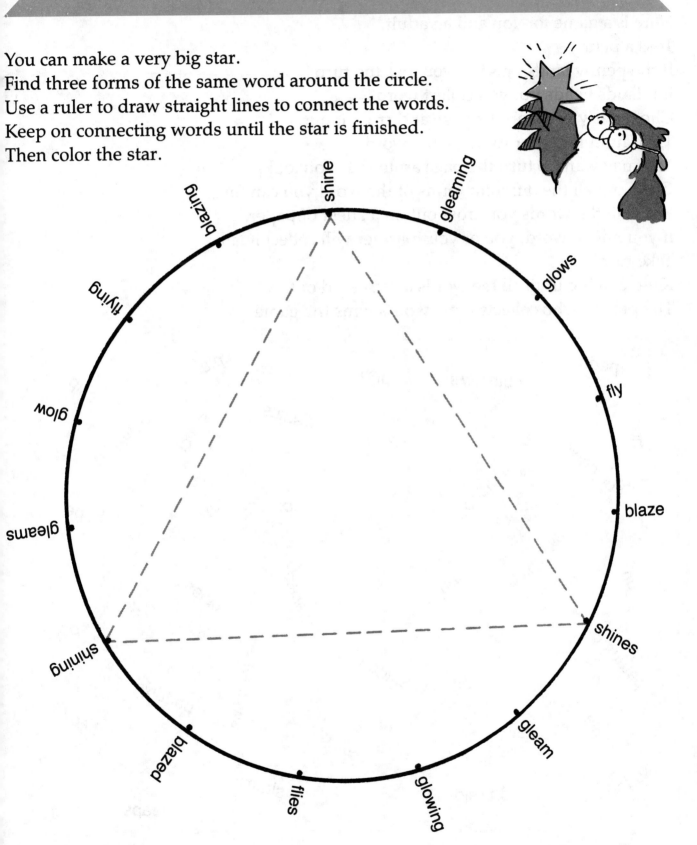

Word Collector

Here is a game for you and an adult.

Toss a penny.

If the penny lands tails up, you lose the turn.

If it lands heads up, you collect words.

Choose any word on the page and cross it out.

Then hunt for other forms of the word.

You may want to turn the page around as you look.

Cross out all the different forms of the word you can find.

Write all the words you cross out on a sheet of paper.

If you miss a word, you or your partner will collect it later.

Take turns.

Keep playing until all the words are crossed out.

The person who collects more words wins the game.

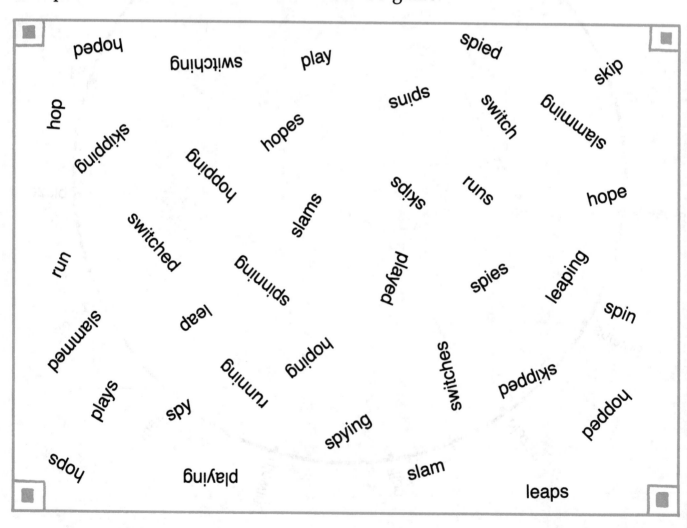

7 Silly Compounds

Read each pair of words at the right.
Say each pair as a regular compound.
The first pair would be **teapot.**
Now make silly compounds by joining the words in different ways.
Join **dog** and **fly** to make **dogfly.**
Write the silly compound dogfly on the line in box **1** below.
Draw a picture in the box to match your idea of a dogfly.
Write a new silly compound in each of the other boxes.
Draw pictures to match your ideas of the silly compounds.

tea	pot
butter	fly
rain	coat
dog	house
sail	boat
paint	brush

My Silly Compounds

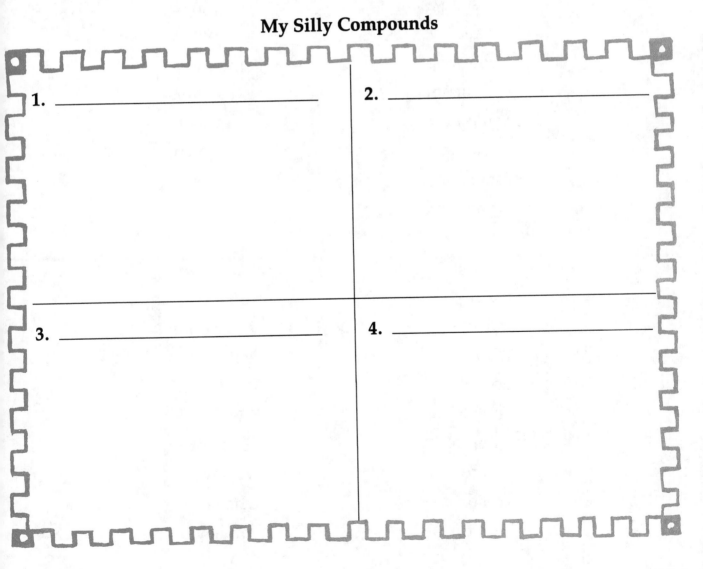

1. _____

2. _____

3. _____

4. _____

Contraction Race

Play this game with a friend.
One player takes the top of the page.
The other player takes the bottom.
Say GO and start drawing lines to connect contractions
with the words that make them up.
The first player to finish says STOP.
If all of that player's lines are correct, the player wins.
If there are mistakes, the player must erase the errors.
Then someone says GO again, and the game continues.
The winner is the first player to match correctly all the words.

you have	won't
who is	you'd
we have	you're
does not	wouldn't
it will	you've
would not	doesn't
will not	who's
you would	it'll
you are	we've

we've	you are
it'll	you would
who's	will not
doesn't	would not
you've	it will
wouldn't	does not
you're	we have
you'd	who is
won't	you have

Follow the Alphabet

What is hiding in this picture?
Connect the words in alphabetical order to find out.
Sometimes two words start with the same letter.
Then look at the second letter before connecting the words.

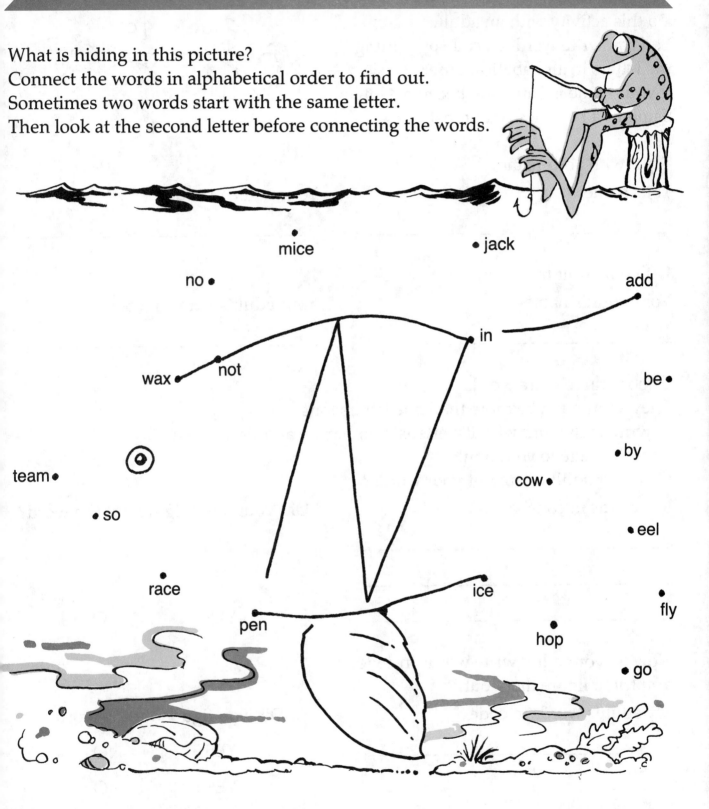

• mice   • jack

no •   add

wax • not   • in

                    be •

team •   • by

• so   cow •

                    • eel

race •   • ice   • fly

pen   hop •

            • go

What did you find hiding in the picture? _____

Alphabet Code

Do this activity with an adult.
You can write words in code by putting the letters in alphabetical order.
If your name is Paul, you become Alpu.
Samantha becomes Aaahmnst.

Fgor   Low

Try it with your name.

Your name   Your name in code

_____   _____

Let your adult try.

Your adult's name   Your adult's name in code

_____   _____

Choose three more words.
They should not be more than five letters long.
Rewrite each word with its letters in alphabetical order.
Give the page to your adult.
Can your adult figure out your words?

My words in code   Did your adult figure out the word?

_____   YES   NO

_____   YES   NO

_____   YES   NO

Now let your adult write words in code.
You try to figure them out.

My adult's words in code   Did you figure out the word?

_____   YES   NO

_____   YES   NO

_____   YES   NO

⑨ Dictionary Mystery

Here are six dictionary entries.
There are pronunciations.
There are the definitions.
There are sample sentences.
The only things missing are the entry words.
Try to add the correct entry words.
Be sure to spell each entry word correctly.

rainbow
(rān´bō)

Entry word

_____

(rōz)
A flower that grows on bushes
and vines.
The red rose smells sweet.

Entry word

_____

(rab´it)
A small animal that has
long ears.
My rabbit can hop.

Entry word

_____

(foks)
A wild animal that lives in
the woods.
The fox hunts for its food.

Entry word

_____

(pē an´ō)
A musical instrument that
has many keys.
I take piano lessons.

Entry word

_____

(lāk)
A body of water that is
surrounded by land.
Let's go swimming in the lake.

Entry word

_____

(bās´bôl´)
A game played with a bat
and a ball.
I am on a baseball team.

Dictionary Numbers

Do this activity with an adult.
Make number cards like these.

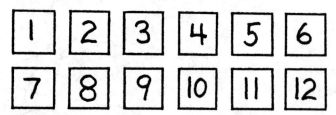

Turn the cards face down and mix them up.
Now read the four dictionary entries below.
Each entry has a pronunciation, a definition, and
a sample sentence.
Choose an entry and look at the numbers in front of
its three parts.
Next, pick three number cards.
If your cards have the same numbers as your entry,
you are a winner.
If your cards do not have the same numbers, return
one of your cards face down.
Mix up the cards again.
Give your adult a turn.
On your next turn, pick one new card and see if you
are a winner now.
Take turns trading in cards until someone is a winner.

pen guin
10 (pen′gwin)
6 An animal that lives
in or near Antarctica.
1 *A penguin is black and
white.*

pup py
12 (pup′ē)
4 A young dog.
5 *The puppy barked.*

por cu pine
2 (pôr′kyə pīn)
3 An animal whose body is
covered with quills.
11 *The porcupine lives in
the woods.*

py thon
9 (pī′thon)
8 A large snake.
7 *I saw a python at the zoo.*

⓪ An Opposites Poem

Read the silly poem below and then rewrite it.
Change every underlined word into an opposite.

In the beautiful land of Goop-dee-goo
   Everyone eats a sweet apple stew.
The boys walk backwards all day long
   And whisper when they sing a song.
The girls are always kind and fair.
   They have big thumbs and long green hair.
It never rains, so remember that—
   You won't need an umbrella or a hat.
Please come along here to Goop-dee-goo,
   We'll all be looking out for you.
                  Peggy Kaye

Rewrite the poem here.

_____

_____

_____

_____

_____

_____

_____

_____

_____

_____

Read the new poem you made.
Which poem do you think is sillier? Circle your answer.   Poem 1   Poem 2

Go Fish

Play this game with an adult.
Make eighteen word cards like these.

quick	fast	slow	friend	cold	enemy
nice	mean	kind	bright	shiny	dull
chilly	pal	hot	easy	hard	simple

Mix up the cards.
Deal four cards to each player.
Spread the rest of the cards face down for a fish pile.
Try for a match of three cards in your hand.
A match must have <u>two</u> cards with words that
mean the same thing (**fast, quick**) and
<u>one</u> card that means the opposite (**slow**).
If you did not have a match from
the deal, ask your adult for a card
that will help you make one.
Your adult must give you any card
that will help you make a match.
Then you may ask for another card.
If your adult does not have a matching
card, she or he says, "Go fish."
You select a card from the fish pile
and then your turn ends.
Now your adult can ask you for a card.
As soon as a player has three matching
cards, they are put on the table and
the player reads the words aloud.
Play until all the cards are matched.
The player with more matches is the winner.

Do you have a match for **cold**?

Yes, I have **hot** and **chilly**.

11 ▸ Which Word?

The sun and its planets move through the Milky Way.
Do you know how fast the sun and planets are moving?
To find out, write the correct word in each sentence.
Look at the number next to the word you chose.
Write that number in the Number Box.
Start at the left and do not skip any spaces.
Add up all the numbers you wrote and
put the sum on the last line in the box.

Come over _____.	hear **10**	here **20**
The wind _____ all night.	blew **25**	blue **15**
I can _____ you.	see **25**	sea **10**
That mouse has a long _____.	tail **15**	tale **10**
We _____ the race!	one **15**	won **30**
Look at my _____ bike.	knew **20**	new **25**
How much does a whale _____?	weigh **20**	way **15**
Put the belt on your _____.	waste **10**	waist **15**

Number Box

_____ + _____ + _____ + _____ + _____ + _____ + _____ + _____ = _____

Complete this sentence with the sum from the Number Box.

The sun and planets travel _____ miles every second!

Riddle Time

This activity is for you and an adult.
Try to answer this riddle.

What is a pony with a cold?

Answer: It is a **hoarse horse**, of course.

How good is your adult at solving riddles?
Read the riddles below to your adult.
Let the adult try to solve each riddle.
Tell your adult that every answer has two words that sound exactly alike.
Circle YES when your adult can solve a riddle.
Circle NO when your adult cannot think of the answer.
You will find the answer below each riddle.

1. What do you call a tired red vegetable?   YES   NO
   Answer   a beat beet

2. What is a simple jetliner?   YES   NO
   Answer   a plain plane

3. What do you call bargain days at a boat store?   YES   NO
   Answer   a sail sale

4. What is a charming woodland animal?   YES   NO
   Answer   a dear deer

5. What do you need to make rose and daisy cake?   YES   NO
   Answer   flower flour

6. What do you call a person who sells basements?   YES   NO
   Answer   a cellar seller

7. What do you call a bit of rabbit fur?   YES   NO
   Answer   hare hair

8. What do you call a light-colored bucket?   YES   NO
   Answer   a pale pail

12 ▶ Word Puzzle

There are two sentences for each word that goes
in the puzzle below.
Try to think of one word that fits both sentences.
Write that word in the puzzle, one letter to a box.

Across

2. You _____ go to the show.
My birthday is on _____ 11th.

3. I _____ a blue bird.
I will _____ the wood.

4. Do not _____ the bus.
My teacher is _____ Jones.

5. _____ me the book.
Look at the clock's big _____.

8. You have dirt on your _____.
A clock has hands and a _____.

9. I will act in a _____.
I want to _____ baseball.

Down

1. Turn on the _____.
The bag feels _____.

2. I know what you _____.
Be nice! Don't be _____.

6. I will _____ the cards.
It is a fair _____.

7. They _____ 1 hour ago.
It is in my _____ hand.

8. The bird can _____.
Don't let the _____ in
the house.

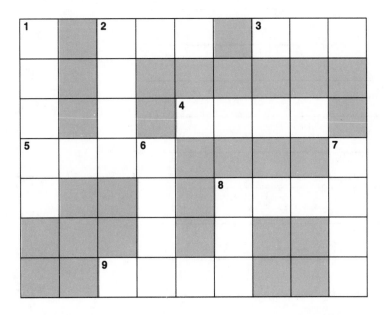

Two Meanings

Do this activity with a friend.
Choose one of the words listed below.
Try to use the word twice in a single sentence.
The sentence must show two different meanings of the word.
Tell your friend your sentence.
Take turns choosing words and making up sentences until you finish the list.
Write your name next to the words you try.
Circle YES if you can make the sentence.
Circle NO if you cannot make the sentence.

Word	Who tried the word?	Did you make a sentence?	
bark	_____	YES	NO
leave	_____	YES	NO
ball	_____	YES	NO
case	_____	YES	NO
duck	_____	YES	NO
jam	_____	YES	NO
fan	_____	YES	NO
mine	_____	YES	NO
fall	_____	YES	NO

③ The Wrong Words

Read this story about a lion and a mouse.
As you read, you will find nine words that do not belong.
Write the words in order at the bottom of the page.

One day in the jungle, a big lion grabbed a little mouse. The lion held the mouse in his paws.

The mouse looked up at the lion and your said, "Please let me go. I am too little to be a good meal. And if you heart let me go, someday I will help you."

The lion laughed, "You help beats me! What a silly idea." The lion one laughed so hard, that it let the mouse slip away. The mouse ran home.

Several weeks hundred passed by. The mouse was at home fixing thousand dinner for his wife. Suddenly, he heard the lion roaring in pain. The mouse ran from his house. He ran through the times woods. He found the lion stuck in a rope trap. The lion every pulled at the ropes, but couldn't get free.

The mouse said, "I'll save you, friend lion."

The little mouse started chewing on the ropes. Soon one rope had a big hole in it. Then another rope had a hole. Then another and another. In a few minutes, the lion was day free. The lion smiled at the mouse and said, "You are little, but you saved the king of the beasts. Thank you, my special friend."

This is a fact. _____ _____ _____

_____ _____ _____ _____

_____ _____!

What's Next?

Give this page to an adult.
Have the adult read you this story about the inventor Thomas Edison.
You may not look at the page.
Some words in the story are underlined.
The adult will stop reading just before saying an underlined word.
You try to guess what word comes next.
You score 2 points if you guess the word.
If you cannot guess, the adult tells you the first letter of the word.
If you can guess the word now, you score 1 point.
Keep score on a piece of paper.

When Thomas Edison was four years <u>old</u>, he was curious about why the family goose spent the entire day sitting on her eggs. His mother explained that a <u>goose</u> sits on her eggs to keep them <u>warm</u>. The eggs must stay warm so that they will <u>hatch</u>.

That afternoon, Tom went out to the barn. Many hours passed. Tom's parents and sister began to worry. What could Tom be doing in the <u>barn</u>? They went to find out.

What do you think they saw? There was Tom curled up in the <u>nest</u>. Tom's father said, "Tom, why are you sitting in a goose nest?"

"I'm hatching eggs," Tom answered.

Tom's sister laughed. "Don't you know anything? You can't hatch <u>eggs</u>."

Tom stood <u>up</u>. Then he saw something. All the eggs were <u>crushed</u>. Tom looked at himself. He was completely covered <u>with</u> yolk. Tom began to <u>cry</u>. That was Thomas Edison's very first experiment.

The highest possible score is 20 points.

How many points did you score? _____

14 ⟩ Who Can It Be?

Think of all the people you know.
Think of friends and relatives.
Think of characters from books, movies, and TV.
Try to think of just the right person
for each sentence below.
When you have the right person in mind,
write the person's name on the blank line.

1. _____ runs as fast as a cheetah.

2. _____ has a voice like a police siren.

3. _____ plays like a silly kitten.

4. _____ can be as quiet as a pillow.

5. _____ is as strong as a polar bear.

6. _____ is as smart as an encyclopedia.

7. _____ is as friendly as a puppy greeting its master.

8. _____ can get as nervous as a rabbit.

9. _____ dresses in colors like a rainbow.

10. _____ can be as sneaky as a fox.

A Monster Story

Have a friend do this activity with you.
Fill in each blank in the story.
You may take turns or work together.
Use words from the Word Box or your own words.

The Monster

A monster just moved in next door. The monster is

nice, but it is as tall as a _____

with hair as green as _____, eyes as

yellow as _____, and skin that feels

like _____. Its voice sounds like

_____.

The monster cooks special food that looks like

_____ and smells like

_____. When the monster is eating,

it sounds like _____.

Yesterday the monster invited me over to play. It

has a ball that is as big as a _____

and a bat that looks like a _____.

I picked up the bat, but it felt as heavy as a

_____. I said, "Let's draw

pictures instead." The monster agreed, so I drew a

picture of the monster, and the monster drew a

picture of me.

You and your friend draw pictures of the monster.
Use separate sheets of paper for your pictures.

Word Box

baby
beach ball
building
crashing cars
crayon
earthquakes
fence posts
fire alarms
frog
gorilla
hay
rotten eggs
house
leaves
mountain
sandpaper
silk
street light
the sun
tree
thunder

5 ▷ This Leads to That

Think of three words that have to do with the word <u>circus</u>.
Write them on these lines.

_____   _____

_____

Choose one of your three words. | A |
Write it in box **A** at the right.
Write three other words that go with the word in box **A**.

_____   _____

_____

Choose a word from your second list. | B |
Write it in box **B** at the right.
Write three other words that go with the word in box **B**.
Do not use any words you used before.

_____   _____

_____

Choose a word from your third list. | C |
Write it in box **C** at the right.
Write three other words that go with the word in box **C**.
Do not use any words you used before.

_____   _____

_____

Look at all the words you wrote.
Try to make a sentence using at least one word
from each of your lists.

_____

_____

Shared Thinking

Have a friend do this activity with you.

For **Round 1**, you and your friend think of the word <u>baseball</u>.

Do not talk to each other.

On this page, write six baseball words that come into your mind.

Your friend writes six words on another sheet of paper.

Do not show each other your papers until you are finished.

When you both are finished, compare your lists.

Score 1 point for every word that is on both lists.

Each of you write your score at the bottom of your own list.

Play **Round 2** for <u>school</u> and **Round 3** for <u>Halloween</u> in the same way.

Round 1 Baseball	**Round 2** School	**Round 3** Halloween
_____	_____	_____
_____	_____	_____
_____	_____	_____
_____	_____	_____
_____	_____	_____
_____	_____	_____
Score _____	**Score** _____	**Score** _____

How many points did you score in all? _____

Eleven to 18 points means you and your friend have thoughts that agree nearly perfectly.

Five to 10 points means you and your friend almost always think alike.

One to 4 points means you and your friend have ideas that are sometimes alike.

Zero means you and your friend are on different wavelengths.

You can do this activity again with three new words or with another partner.

6 Class Partners

Welcome to Animal School.

Everyone in Animal School must have a partner.

Here is how to find yours.

The animals in this class are in two groups.

Read all the signs in both groups.

Signs in **Group A** are sentence beginnings.

Signs in **Group B** are sentence endings.

Try to match each sentence beginning with its correct ending.

Draw lines between the matching signs.

When you are finished, the one animal in Group A without

a sentence ending will be your partner for the day.

Group A   **Group B**

Red is to stop

Car is to road

Hit is to baseball

Read is to book

Rain is to drop

Apple is to tree

as train is to track.

as green is to go.

as kick is to football.

as listen is to radio.

as eggs are to hens.

Who is your class partner for the day? _____

The Right Words

This is a game to play with a friend.
Here are twenty-one words.
Choose eight words for yourself and underline them.
Have your friend choose eight different words and circle them.

table	snow	foot	winter	bowl	hot	fire
paper	lane	clown	mouse	tiger	clock	milk
rink	nose	button	book	circle	spoon	electricity

Work with your friend to complete the sentences below.
You score 1 point every time you use an underlined word.
Your friend scores 1 point every time you use a circled word.
Keep track of your points on another sheet of paper.

Chalk is to board as pencil is to _____.

Glove is to hand as shoe is to _____.

August is to summer as January is to _____.

Swimming is to pool as ice-skating is to _____.

Milk is to glass as soup is to _____.

Ice is to cold as steam is to _____.

Sheep is to wool as cow is to _____.

Cars are to gas as lamps are to _____.

Baseball is to field as bowling is to _____.

Shoe is to lace as coat is to _____.

How many points did you score? _____

How many points did your friend score? _____

7 You Be the Judge

Pam and Kana entered a writing contest.
Each hopes that her paragraph is the best.
You be the judge.
Read each paragraph.
Remember a good paragraph has one main idea.
All the sentences in the paragraph should be
filled with information about that idea.

Pam's Paragraph

A volcano is an opening in the earth. When the earth
opens, gas and rock shoot up into the air from deep
inside the earth. I have never seen a volcano. The rock is
melted. It has a special name. My nickname is Pammy.
The rock is called magma. When magma comes out of
the volcano it is called lava.

Kana's Paragraph

When the lava hardens it becomes rocks. There are
many kinds of lava rocks. A block is a lava rock with
sharp corners. A bomb is a round piece of lava rock. A
cinder is a very light rock. The lightest lava rock of all is
called pumice. Pumice rock is so light it floats on water.

Who should win the first prize ribbon? _____

What is the main idea of the first prize paragraph?

_____

_____

_____

_____

Sentence Match

Play this game with a friend.

At the bottom of the page are two main ideas for a paragraph, one for you and one for a friend.

You must match your main idea with sentences from the Sentence List.

Make number cards like those at the right.

Mix up the cards and turn them face down.

Take turns picking a card.

The card you pick tells you which sentence you get from the list.

If the sentence matches your main idea, write the number under your main idea.

If it does not, put the card back.

The winner is the first player to match four sentences to his or her main idea.

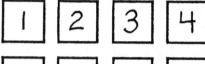

Sentence List

1. An elephant's trunk is also its nose.
2. Giraffes are so tall, they can see enemies from far away.
3. Its skin color helps it to hide in the trees and grass.
4. There is a finger on the end of the nose.
5. The nose is so strong it can pull down trees.
6. It can kick an enemy with its long legs.
7. To take a shower, an elephant fills its nose with water.
8. It can hit an enemy with its strong neck.

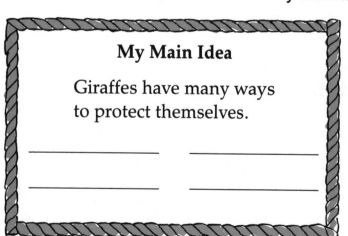

My Main Idea

Giraffes have many ways to protect themselves.

_____ _____

_____ _____

My Friend's Main Idea

Elephants have the most amazing noses.

_____ _____

_____ _____

Letter Change

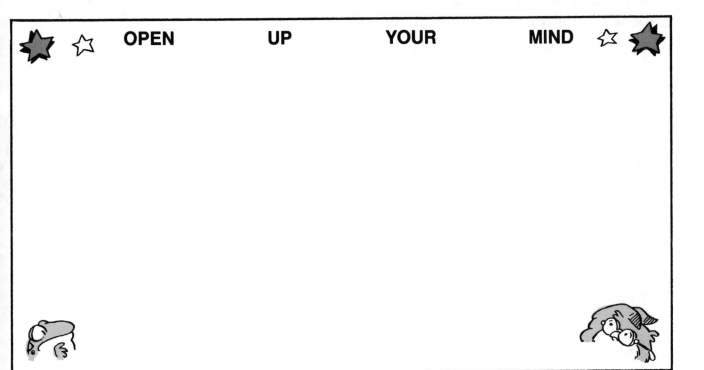

OPEN   UP   YOUR   MIND

Follow the directions below.
You will OPEN UP YOUR MIND to another message.
Each time you change a letter or letters in a word,
rewrite the new spelling below the word that is changed.

1. Switch P and N in the first word.

2. Change all the vowels in the last two words to O.

3. Change the first and last letters of the whole message to K.

4. Change M to W.

5. Add the word THE between the second and third words.

6. Change R to D.

7. Change the first N to E and the last N to R.

8. Change Y to G.

Write your new message here.

_____ _____ _____ _____ _____

Do As I Say

Ask a friend to play this game.
Choose one of the sets of instructions below.
Read the instructions to your friend.
When you finish reading, have your friend try to follow the
instructions in order without looking at the page.
If your friend follows them correctly, write his or her name in the box.
If your friend cannot follow them, leave the box blank.
Then have your friend choose a set of instructions for you to follow.
Keep playing until you have names in all six boxes.

Banana,
Banana

Set 1
Stand up.
Touch your toes three times.
Turn around.
Shout, "Hello!"

_____

Set 4
Sit on the floor.
Clap your hands once.
Rub your tummy.
Pull on your ears.

_____

Set 2
Skip to the nearest door.
Knock on the door.
Say, "Surprise!"
Jump up in the air.

_____

Set 5
Make a silly face.
Say, "Banana, banana."
Touch your nose with
your thumb.

_____

Set 3
Hum a tune.
Put both hands in the air.
Growl like a dog.
Blink your eyes three times.

_____

Set 6
Touch one knee with both hands.
Jump two times.
Say, "I'm hungry!"
Stamp your feet.

_____

⑨ **Whose Restaurant?**

Here are menus from three different restaurants.
One restaurant is for monsters. It is called Monster Cafe.
One restaurant is for babies. It is called Baby Bits.
One restaurant is for sports stars. It is called Fitness Food.
The restaurants' names are missing from the menus.
Read each menu. Write the restaurant's name at the top.
Then add today's special dish at the bottom.

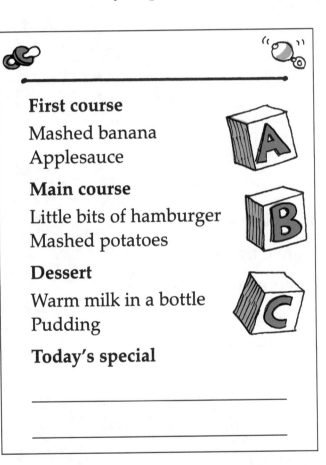

First course
Mashed banana
Applesauce

Main course
Little bits of hamburger
Mashed potatoes

Dessert
Warm milk in a bottle
Pudding

Today's special

_____

_____

First course
Worm dumpling
Eye of bat soup

Main course
Spider stew
Fried lion's paw

Dessert
Paste and dirt pie
Twig and leaf cake

Today's special

_____

_____

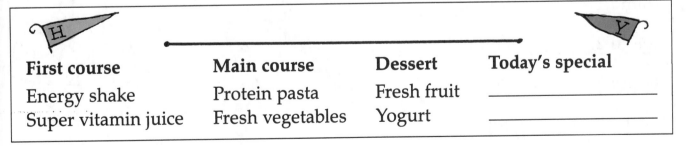

First course
Energy shake
Super vitamin juice

Main course
Protein pasta
Fresh vegetables

Dessert
Fresh fruit
Yogurt

Today's special

_____

_____

What Is My Job?

Play this game with an adult.
Look at the lists of jobs below.
Pick one of them or choose any other job you want.
Do not tell your adult which one you chose.
Tell three things about the job, but do not give its name.
Here is an example.

> You come to me when you are hungry.
> I sell fruits, vegetables, and other kinds of food.
> When you finish visiting me, you go home with
> a bag full of good things to eat.
> What is my job?

If your adult can guess the job, score 1 point.
Take turns.
Play three rounds and keep score in the Score Box.

JOBS

a cook	a carpenter	a ballet dancer
a doctor	a bank teller	an animal trainer
a plumber	a fire fighter	a pet store owner
a teacher	a mail carrier	a shoe salesperson
a musician	a window washer	a newspaper reporter

Score Box	
Me	**My Adult**
Round 1	Round 1
Round 2	Round 2
Round 3	Round 3
Total	Total

What Will Happen?

Here is part of a story about Julian who has a loose tooth.

"Well," my father said, "if you wait long enough, it will fall out." He was talking about my tooth, my right bottom front tooth.

"How long do I have to wait?" I asked. Because I had *two* right bottom front teeth—one firm little new one pushing in, and one wiggly old one.

"I can't say," my father said. "Maybe a month, maybe two months. Maybe less."

"I don't want to wait," I said. "I want *one* tooth there, and I don't want to wait two months!"

"All right!" said my father. "I'll take care of it!" He jumped out of his chair and ran out the door to the garage. He was back in a minute, carrying something—a pair of pliers!

"Your tooth is a little loose already," my father said. "So I'll just put the pliers in your mouth for a second, twist, and the tooth will come out. You won't feel a thing!"

"I won't feel a thing?" I looked at the pliers—huge, black-handled pliers with a long pointed tip. I thought I *would* feel a thing. I thought it would hurt.

"Shall I?" said my dad. He raised the pliers toward my mouth.

What do you think will happen next?
Write your ideas here or on another sheet of paper.

_____

_____

Do you want to know what really happens?
You can find out in the book *The Stories Julian Tells* by Ann Cameron.

Problems, Problems

Ask an adult to work on these problems with you.

My Problems

Read this problem to yourself.

You are in a food store. You want to pay for the food, but you forgot your money at home. What do you do?

Read these three plans.
Underline the plan that tells what you would do.

1. Go home and get money.
2. Ask the storekeeper to wait for the money.
3. Phone a friend to bring money.

Now read the same problem and plans to your adult.
Circle the choice your adult picks.

Read this problem to yourself.

Your favorite TV show is on, but your TV is not working. What do you do?

Read these three plans.
Underline the plan that tells what you would do.

1. Forget the show for tonight.
2. Visit a friend and watch the show there.
3. Try to fix the TV.

Now read the same problem and plans to your adult.
Circle the choice your adult picks.

My Adult's Problem

Let your adult have a turn reading this problem and its plans with you.

You are rushing to get ready for school and juice spills on your homework. What do you do?

1. Give the teacher the homework with juice stains on it.
2. Redo the homework before school starts.
3. Leave the homework at home and tell the teacher what happened.

Now write the number of the plan that tells what you would do. _____

My adult thought I would pick plan number _____.

21 ▶ Crime Buster

Mrs. Glow's biggest diamond is missing.
Here are four police reports.
Read each one.
Then fill in the Crime Buster Sheet.

Police Log   Captain Smith

8:15 PM - Mrs. Glow called to report a stolen diamond. Three diamond thieves are in town - Diamond Bugs, Diamond Stan, and Unlucky Lou. I sent Detectives Shin, Gomez, and Foster to investigate.

Police Log   Detective Shin

7:30 PM - Last time Mrs. Glow saw the diamond.
7:50 PM - Butler heard noises in Mrs. Glow's room.
8:00 PM - Cook saw a red car speeding away from house.

Police Log   Detective Foster

Bugs and Stan drive red cars. Lou has a blue car.
7:00 - 8:30 PM - Bugs had dinner at the Drippy Diner and then left.
8:30 PM - Lou walked in and took a seat.

Police Log   Detective Gomez

4:00 PM - Stan went to store to buy a present for his wife's birthday.
4:30 - 9:30 PM - Stan was at wife's party.
5:00 PM - Lou borrowed Stan's car.
10:00 PM - Lou returned Stan's car and gave flowers to Stan's wife.

Crime Buster Sheet

1. What time was the robbery? _____

2. What color car was the robber driving? _____

3. Who has that color car? _____

4. What was Bugs doing at the time of the robbery? _____

5. What was Stan doing at the time of the robbery? _____

6. Who was driving Stan's car? _____

7. What was Lou doing? _____

8. Whom should Police Captain Smith arrest? _____

Pyramids

Do this with a friend.
How was a pyramid built by the Egyptians of long ago?
It was hard work, and it took many years.
Here are four different pyramid building plans.
Only one plan gives the correct order for building a pyramid.
Read each plan.
Decide which plan is in correct order.

1. The land is measured.
   The desert is cleared.
   The pointed stone is set on top.
   The stones are put in place.
   The stones are polished.

2. The desert is cleared.
   The land is measured.
   The stones are put in place.
   The pointed stone is set on top.
   The stones are polished.

3. The desert is cleared.
   The stones are put in place.
   The land is measured.
   The stones are polished.
   The pointed stone is set on top.

4. The stones are put in place.
   The pointed stone is set on top.
   The stones are polished.
   The land is measured.
   The desert is cleared.

Which plan do you think is correct?   1   2   3   4

Which plan does your friend think is correct?   1   2   3   4

Which way is correct?
Answer this upside down question, and you will find out.

—————— How many shoes are in a pair? ——————

That is the correct plan number for pyramid building.

22 > Three Poems

Read each poem. Then answer the question below it.

Way Down South

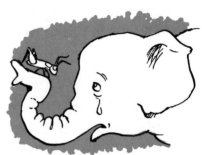

Way down South where bananas grow,
A grasshopper stepped on an elephant's toe.
The elephant said with tears in his eyes,
"Pick on somebody your own size!"

What nonsense is in this poem? _____

_____

As I Was Going Out

As I was going out one day
My head fell off and rolled away.
But when I saw that it was gone,
I picked it up and put it on.

And when I got into the street
A fellow cried: "Look at your feet!"
I looked at them and sadly said:
"I've left them both asleep in bed!"

What is silly in this poem? _____

_____

Hullabaloo

I raised a great hullabaloo
When I found a large mouse in my stew,
  Said the waiter, "Don't shout
  And wave it about,
Or the rest will be wanting one, too!"

Why is this poem funny? _____

_____

Air and Water

This activity is for you to do with an adult.
Read these statements together.

1. Oceans and seas take up about $\frac{2}{3}$ of the earth's surface.
2. The average person uses 168 gallons of water a day.
3. You can live for two weeks without food, two days without water, but only several minutes without air.
4. One molecule out of every 500 molecules of air you breathe has been exhaled by another person.
5. A single car produces more than a ton of harmful gases each year.

Circle the statements you think are true. 1 2 3 4 5

Circle the statements your adult thinks are true. 1 2 3 4 5

Now read the two paragraphs below.
Statements 1, 3, and 5 are true if everything in both paragraphs makes sense.
Statements 2 and 4 are true if everything in one paragraph makes sense but there is nonsense in the other.
All the statements are true if both paragraphs have nonsense.

1. We all need clean air to breathe, but it is hard to keep our air clean. Cars, machines, and factories all create bad gases that dirty the air. Scientists must work hard to find new ways to make our air hard to breathe. Our government has laws telling companies to keep our air as clean as possible. Working together, we can make sure that we always have clean air to breathe.

2. Water pollution is another bad problem. How can we keep our waters polluted and unsafe for fish, people, animals, and plants? Governments all over the world must act together to protect the oceans. Businesses must develop ways to protect our waterways, too. We must all help to keep the water clean.

How I Felt

Remember a time you felt excited.
What happened to make you feel excited?

_____

_____

_____

Remember a time you laughed.
What happened to make you laugh?

_____

_____

_____

Remember a time you felt surprised.
What happened to make you feel surprised?

_____

_____

_____

Remember a time you felt smart.
What happened to make you feel smart?

_____

_____

_____

Remember a time you felt proud.
What happened to make you feel proud?

_____

_____

_____

What Happened?

Ask a friend to do this activity with you.
Read each story and decide why things happened.
Write your reason.
Then have your friend write a different reason.

Mrs. King opened her refrigerator because she wanted some juice. All the juice was gone. There was nothing left but an empty bottle. Mrs. King was surprised. What could have happened?

My idea _____

_____

My friend's idea _____

_____

Ruth is the best player on the baseball team. Ruth told the coach she could not play in the big game. The coach was surprised. What could have happened?

My idea _____

_____

My friend's idea _____

_____

The Cruz family sat down for dinner. Then, before eating, everyone got up from the table. They left the house, got in the car, and drove to a restaurant. What could have happened?

My idea _____

_____

My friend's idea _____

_____

The Wrong Side

Read this story about a girl named Jody.

The Wrong Side

"Time for breakfast," Jody's mom called.

"I'm coming. Stop rushing me," Jody shouted. She finished combing her hair and picked up her notebook. The book fell and her papers tumbled out. "I hate my notebook. Everything falls out of it."

Jody's mom hurried in to help. "This is easy to fix," she said as she picked up the papers. "There, now everything is in order. Come to breakfast. I made pancakes, your favorite."

"I don't want pancakes," Jody grumbled.

Just then, Jody's baby brother crawled into the room. "Kiss, kiss," he said when he saw his big sister.

"Go away, Ned. I'm busy," Jody shouted.

The little boy began to cry.

"Jody," her mother said, "You certainly got up on the wrong side of the bed this morning."

"What does that mean?" Jody asked.

"It means you are in a bad mood. It means everything is making you angry today."

Jody lay down on her bed. "I'll start today over. This time I'll get up on the right side of the bed."

Pretend Jody woke up in a good mood this morning. Write *two* things that would be different in the story.

_____

_____

_____

_____

Switching Places

Do this activity with an adult.
This part is for you.
Name five things you would do if you were an adult. 1ˢᵗ 2ⁿᵈ 3ʳᵈ 4ᵗʰ 5ᵗʰ

First, I would _____

_____

Second, I would _____

_____

Third, I would _____

_____

Fourth, I would _____

_____

Fifth, I would _____

_____

This part is for your adult.
Name five things you would do if you were a child.

First, I would _____

_____

Second, I would _____

_____

Third, I would _____

_____

Fourth, I would _____

_____

Fifth, I would _____

_____

What's Wrong?

Read this story about Edmund Elf and then study the picture.
On the lines below the picture, list six things that are
wrong in the picture because they do not match the story.

Edmund Elf lived with his parents, grandparents, and fourteen older brothers and sisters. Edmund hated being the youngest. Everyone bossed him around. He decided to run away from home. Edmund put on his polka dotted shirt and his striped pants. He packed his backpack with his favorite books. Edmund also took his magic ring. With this ring, Edmund could make any wish come true. Then Edmund set off down the road.

Edmund walked until he came to a two story house. Three children were in the yard. They invited Edmund to play. Edmund showed the children his magic ring. The children made wonderful wishes. They wished for a tree house, a cat, and a monkey. Every wish came true. Then the sun began to set. The children begged the little elf to stay and live with them forever. But Edmund was feeling lonely. He missed his mother, his father, and his grandparents. He even missed his brothers and sisters. So Edmund made one more wish that day. Edmund wished to go home.

Things Wrong in the Picture

1. _____

2. _____

3. _____

4. _____

5. _____

6. _____

A Visitor

Do this activity with an adult.
Earth has a visitor.
It is a space traveler from the planet Zygryz.
Here is a description of the Zygryzian.
Read the description aloud to your adult.
Then draw a picture on this page to fit the description.
Have your adult draw a picture on separate paper.
Do not look at each other's drawings until you are finished.
If the adult needs you to reread the description,
you must do it.
When you are finished, compare your drawings.

I'd like to meet that Zygryzian.

It must need a lot of hats in the winter.

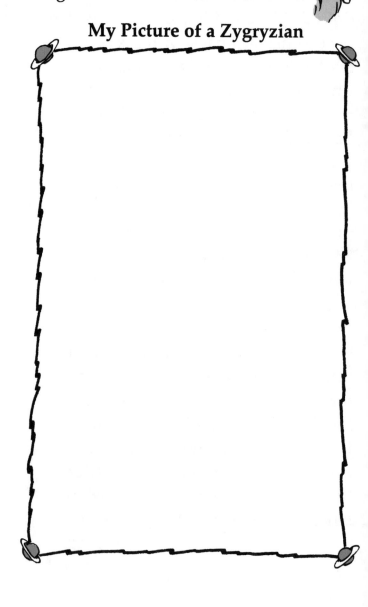

My Picture of a Zygryzian

The Zygryzian has two orange heads. It has one eye in the middle of each head. It has one antenna on its left head. It has a mouth on the forehead of its left head and a nose on the forehead of its right head. It has long curly yellow hair on its left head and short straight blue hair on its right head. It has two long thin gray necks that meet at a huge fat body. Its body is striped green and purple. It has two pink legs and four red arms with three fingers on each fat hand.

Black Holes

You already know information that can help you understand black holes in space.
Write one fact you know about our sun.

_____

Write one fact you know about stars.

_____

Write one fact you know about gravity.

_____

Now read this story about black holes.

When you look at the night sky, you see many stars. The stars look like little bits of light, but that is only because they are so far away. One star is very close to the earth. That star is our sun.

All stars, our sun included, are made of very hot gases. The hot gas moves very fast. Sometimes stars begin to cool. As the stars begin to cool, the gas moves more slowly. Gravity pulls the gases to the center of a star and packs the gases very close together. The star becomes very small and the gases are so close together that no light can escape. That is when a star becomes a black hole.

Gravity from the black hole is so strong that it pulls gases from other stars into its center. The black hole can actually pull neighboring stars apart. Gases in the hole are so close together that one thimbleful weighs billions of tons.

Will our sun ever become a black hole? Maybe, but not for billions and billions of years.

What is one new thing you learned from this story?

_____

Getting to Know You

Do this activity for a friend.
How well do you know your friend?
Fill in the Getting to Know You form.

I didn't know you liked green beans!

Getting to Know You

Write three things your friend does during free time.

1. _____

2. _____

3. _____

Write three animals your friend likes.

1. _____

2. _____

3. _____

Write three things your friend likes to eat.

1. _____

2. _____

3. _____

Write three things your friend would like as gifts.

1. _____

2. _____

3. _____

Read your ideas to your friend.
How many times did your friend agree with your ideas? _____

27 ▶ Solve the Problem

Here are parts of two different story plans.
Each one names the story's characters.
Each one tells where the story takes place, or the **setting**.
Each one gives a problem.
You must think of a way to solve each problem.

PLAN 1

The characters   An eight year old girl named Rosa
                     Rosa's grandmother

The setting   Grandmother's house late at night

The problem   Rosa is living with Grandmother while her
                  parents are away on a trip.
                  Late one night, Grandmother becomes very sick.
                  Grandmother is in her bed and cannot move.
                  She calls for Rosa.

What will Rosa do? _____

_____

_____

PLAN 2

The characters   A kind wizard
                     A mean ogre
                     A boy named Carlos

The setting   Deep in a forest

The problem   The wizard has a magic wand.
                  All of his magic is in the wand.
                  The ogre steals the wand.
                  The wizard asks Carlos to help get the wand back.

What will Carlos do? _____

_____

_____

Spin a Tale

This activity is for you and a friend.
Make number cards like these.

Put the cards face down and mix them up.
Turn over three cards and put them in a row.
The number on the first card tells you which
problem to solve.
Work together with your friend to invent a story to
solve the problem.
Use the character with the same number as the second card.
Use the setting with the same number as the third card.
Take turns adding parts to the story.
Be as silly as you like.
When you are finished, turn over your cards and mix them
up with the rest of the cards.
Then have your friend turn over three cards.
Work together to invent another story.
If the same problem, character, or setting comes up, try
to use it in a different story.
After you finish your second story, decide which story
you both liked better.
On separate paper, draw pictures to go with the story.

Problem	Character	Setting
1. A character is on a sinking ship.	1. a talking cat	1. the beach
2. A character turns invisible.	2. a dragon	2. a science lab
3. A character meets a mean bully.	3. a tiny baby	3. a schoolyard
4. A character is caught in an earthquake.	4. the tooth fairy	4. a mountain top

A True Story

When you study history, you learn about the past.
You learn about events and people from another time.
This story about Lydia Darragh is part of our American history.

In the year 1777, The Americans and the British were
fighting against one another in the American
Revolutionary War. General George Washington was the
leader of the American army. Lydia Darragh was a spy
who helped General Washington.

The British held meetings in Lydia's home. They made
war plans. They did not pay any attention to Lydia, but
that was their mistake.

One night, the British told Lydia they needed her
house for a meeting. Lydia hid in a closet and listened.
She heard the British plan a surprise attack on the
Americans. She knew she had to tell Washington. The
next day, Lydia walked for many hours in the freezing
cold to reach General Washington's troops. She told
them about the attack. Then she walked back home.

Because of Lydia, General Washington was ready
when the British attacked. The British lost the battle.
Thanks to brave Lydia Darragh and many people like
her, the Americans won the Revolutionary War.

Think about Lydia and the kind of person she was.

Write one way you are like Lydia. _____

_____

Write one way you are different from Lydia. _____

_____

If you could talk to Lydia, what would you say to her? _____

_____

Number Tricks

Have a friend do these tricks with you.

Trick 1

Tell your friend to write a number between 1 and 9
on a sheet of paper.
Your friend must not let you see this number or the math
work to come.
Tell your friend to multiply the number by 3.
Next add 2.
Then multiply the new number by 3.
Tell your friend to add the first number to the result.
Your friend should now tell you this final number.
Write the number here.

If your friend did the math correctly, this will be a two
digit number with a 6 in the ones place.
Cross off the 6.
The remaining number is your friend's secret number.

Trick 2

Tell your friend to write any number he or she wants
on a sheet of paper.
You must not see your friend's number or math work.
Tell your friend to add 9 to the number.
Next, double the new number.
Then subtract 4.
Next, divide the new number by 2.
Finally, subtract the first number from the result.
Now, announce to your friend that the number
on his or her page is 7.
If your friend did the math correctly, 7 will always be
the answer.

It's the News

Here is a newspaper story for you to finish.
You may make yourself the star of the story
or you may use any other name you want.
Write all the information needed to tell the news.

A Surprise Winner

Yesterday the town of _____ held its yearly

_____ contest at _____ in the afternoon.

Everyone was surprised when _____ took first place in the

_____ contest. To win the contest _____

had to _____ and _____ and

_____. After the contest, the winner felt _____.

The winner believed this success was due to _____.

The winner said, "_____

_____."

Some of the other contestants felt _____. One of them

said, "_____

_____."

If you want to be in the contest next year, you must _____

_____.

It will also help if you _____

_____.

Story Notes

Play this game with a friend or family member.
Make number cards like these.
Turn the cards face down and mix them up.
Now you will take notes for a newspaper story.
You have to know **who** the story is about, **what** happened,
when it happened, **where** it happened, and **why** it happened.
Take turns picking a card.
The number on the card tells you which box you win from
the News Pool.
Write the information from the box in your Story Notes below.
If you do not need a card, return it face down.
The winner is the first player who completes the story notes.

1	2	3	4
5	6	7	
8	9	10	

News Pool

1 Who	2 What	3 When	4 Where	5 Why
Molly Mouse	spilled the milk	last Monday	in the kitchen	she was looking for cheese
6 Who	7 What	8 When	9 Where	10 Why
Karen Cat	had babies	yesterday	in a sock drawer	she wanted a quiet, warm spot

My Story Notes

Who _____

What _____

When _____

Where _____

Why _____

_____

My Friend's Story Notes

Who _____

What _____

When _____

Where _____

Why _____

_____

Poem Day

You can write a poem about animals.
Use words from the Word List to finish the sentences.
You may use any other words you want.

Animal Poem

Puppies _____

Cats _____

Fish _____

Birds _____

Hamsters _____

Lions _____

Lambs _____

Monkeys _____

Bears _____.

Word List

scamper	whimper
swish	leap
dive	growl
spin	bubble
soar	flash
purr	stamp
jump	climb
sing	roam
chatter	cuddle
scratch	claw
lick	sniff

Work on a new poem about an imaginary secret pal.
Read all the words in the poem below.
Keep the words that tell about your pal.
Cross out the words that do not tell about your pal.
Add three new words of your own.

My Secret Pal

My pal is
Silly, lively, jumpy, serious,
Jolly, noisy, sneaky, smart,
Flashy, strong, delightful,
Daring, thoughtful, calm,
Polite, sparkly, snuggly,

_____, _____, _____.

A Pocket's Poem

Read this poem to a friend.
When you are finished, fill in your Idea Sheet.
Then have your friend fill in his or her idea sheet.

Keep a Poem in Your Pocket

Keep a poem in your pocket
and a picture in your head
and you'll never feel lonely
at night when you're in bed.

The little poem will sing to you
the little picture bring to you
a dozen dreams to dance to you
at night when you're in bed.

So—
Keep a picture in your pocket
and a poem in your head
and you'll never feel lonely
at night when you're in bed.

Beatrice Schenk de Regniers

My Idea Sheet

Before I go to sleep, I like to _____

_____

_____

At night it would be fun to dream

about _____

_____

_____

My Friend's Idea Sheet

Before I go to sleep, I like to _____

_____

_____

At night it would be fun to dream

about _____

_____

_____

31 ▶ Trick an Ogre

In the story *Puss In Boots*, a clever cat named Puss
tricks an ogre.
The ogre claims it can turn itself into any animal on earth.
Puss asks, "Can you turn yourself into a lion?"
The ogre laughs and turns into the king of beasts.
Then Puss asks, "Can you turn yourself into an elephant?"
The ogre laughs and turns into the huge animal.
Puss says, "You can turn yourself into the biggest of
creatures, but can you turn yourself into a tiny mouse?"
The ogre says, "Of course I can, just watch."
As soon as the ogre turns into a mouse, Puss leaps
on it and eats it up.

How would you trick an ogre?
Choose an idea from the Problem Box or use your own idea.
On the lines below, write a story about how you would solve
the problem by tricking the ogre.

Problem Box

The ogre doesn't want to let you pass its home.

The ogre won't let you have a drink of water from its well.

You need food, but the ogre won't share its bread and soup.

_____

_____

_____

_____

_____

_____

_____

That's Impossible

Do this activity with a friend.
In a tall tale, the storyteller boasts about the characters.
Paul Bunyan is a character in a tall tale.
Here are some of the boasts made about him.

I'm so strong I can lift up an apartment house!

Paul Bunyan was bigger than a house.
When he sneezed, he blew birds out of the air.
Paul was so big he carried trees around in his pockets.
When Paul was a baby, he tossed in his sleep and
knocked down a mile of trees.
Paul had a pancake griddle so huge that a crew
of men strapped bacon slabs to their feet
and skated on the griddle to get it greased.

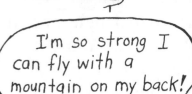

I'm so strong I can fly with a mountain on my back!

Have a boasting contest with your friend.
Make a huge, fantastic boast about yourself.
Make it a boast that could not possibly be true.
Then challenge your friend to out-boast you.

1. **My Boast**   I am so strong that _____

_____

My Friend's Boast   I am so strong that _____

_____

2. **My Boast**   I am so fast that _____

_____

My Friend's Boast   I am so fast that _____

_____

3. **My Boast**   I hear so well that _____

_____

My Friend's Boast   I hear so well that _____

_____

More. . .
It's the news

Here is a newspaper story for you to finish.
You may make yourself the star of the story
or you may use any other name you want.
Write all the information needed to tell the news.

A Surprise Winner

Yesterday the town of _____ held its yearly

_____ contest at _____ in the afternoon.

Everyone was surprised when _____ took first place in the

_____ contest. To win the contest _____

had to _____ and _____ and

_____. After the contest, the winner felt _____.

The winner believed this success was due to _____.

The winner said, "_____

_____."

Some of the other contestants felt _____. One of them

said, "_____

_____."

If you want to be in the contest next year, you must _____

_____.

It will also help if you _____

_____

_____.

Enrichment
Reading Grade 4

AMERICAN
EDUCATION
PUBLISHING

1 Word Detective

List eight objects you find in your classroom or your home.
Next to each object, write the first describing word you think
of when you look at the object.

Then write a word that means the same or almost the same
as the describing word.

Finally, write a word that means the opposite of the
describing word.

Object	Describing Word	Same	Opposite
table	hard	solid	soft
1.			
2.			
3.			
4.			
5.			
6.			
7.			
8.			

Wonder Wheel

Here is a game to play with an adult.
Make ten word cards like these.
Put the cards in a pile and turn the pile face down.
Take the top card and read the word.
Then toss a penny onto the Wonder Wheel.
If it lands on **S**, say a word that means the same as the word on the card.
If it lands on **O**, say a word that means the opposite of the word on the card.
If both players agree a word is right, score 5 points.
Then return the card to the bottom of the pile.
Take turns and keep score on a piece of paper.
Play until one player scores 30 points.

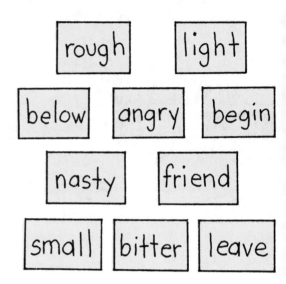

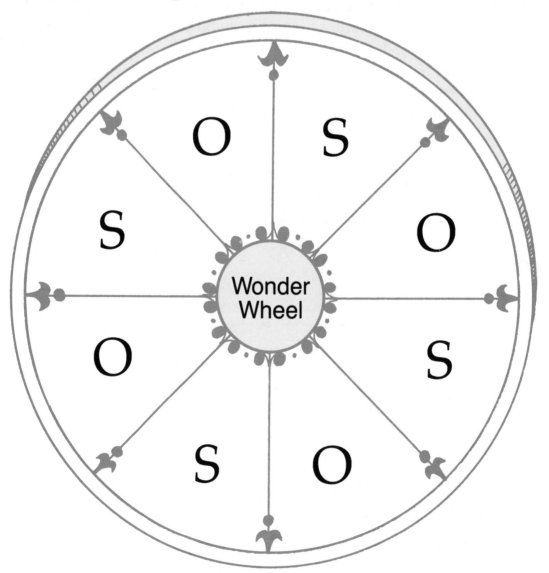

Name _____

2 Jungle Maze

Help the explorer find her way through the jungle.
Use a pencil to follow the path of words with prefixes.
Be careful, or the explorer will be lost forever.

Prefix Puzzle

Ask someone to play this game with you.
Toss a penny or paper clip onto the puzzle.
Read the word on which it lands.
If the word has one prefix, score 5 points.
If the word has two prefixes, score 10 points.
If the word has no prefixes, your score is 0.
Take turns and play six rounds. Keep score below.
The player with the higher score wins.

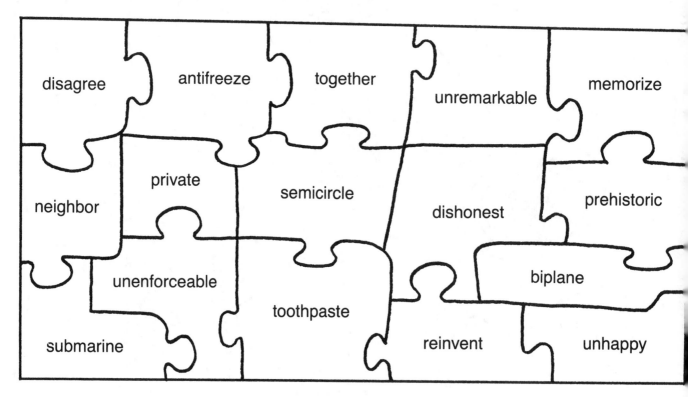

disagree   antifreeze   together   unremarkable   memorize

neighbor   private   semicircle   dishonest   prehistoric

unenforceable   toothpaste   biplane

submarine   reinvent   unhappy

Score Sheet	
Player 1	**Player 2**
Round 1	Round 1
Round 2	Round 2
Round 3	Round 3
Round 4	Round 4
Round 5	Round 5
Round 6	Round 6
TOTAL	TOTAL

Message Wall

The bricklayer needs help completing the message on the wall.
Each brick on the ground contains a different suffix.
Write the correct suffix in each empty space.
Cross out the suffix after you use it.

To	beauti		your	block	you	do	not
need	a	paint		or	magic		Just
work	out	a	reason		plan	that	will
keep	your	neighbor		clean,	not	mess	

| able | fy | er | y | hood | ian |

What does the message say?
List three things for a plan to keep your neighborhood clean.

_____

_____

_____

Did You Know?

Play this game with a friend or an adult.
Make eight suffix cards like these.

| est | ance | ly | ing | ment | y | less | ed |

Turn the cards face down.
Choose a card.
If the suffix on the card completes the unfinished word in
one of your sentences, write the suffix on the blank and keep
the card.
If you cannot use the suffix, turn the card back over.
Take turns.
The first player to complete all four sentences is the winner.

Player 1 _____

The discover_____ of dinosaur
bones in England in 1822 was a great
surprise.

The fear_____ Tyrannosaurs were
savage meat eaters.

Scientists general_____ agree that
dinosaurs are more closely related to
birds than to reptiles.

The disappear_____ of dinosaurs
may have been caused by a change in
the earth's climate.

Player 2 _____

There is disagree_____ on
whether dinosaurs were cold-blooded,
like reptiles, or warm-blooded, like
birds.

The long_____ known dinosaur
to ever live was 90 feet long.

Scientists learn about dinosaurs by
study_____ the preserved bones,
teeth, eggs, and tracks of dinosaurs.

Some museums have create_____
realistic models of dinosaurs out of
metal, wire, and screen.

4 ▸ Space Trip

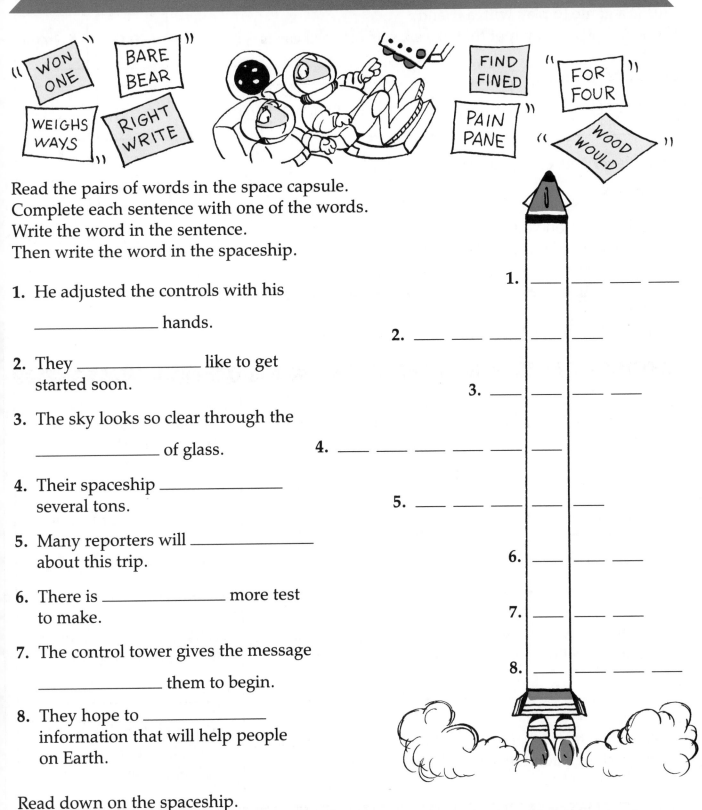

Read the pairs of words in the space capsule.
Complete each sentence with one of the words.
Write the word in the sentence.
Then write the word in the spaceship.

1. He adjusted the controls with his

   _____ hands.

2. They _____ like to get
   started soon.

3. The sky looks so clear through the

   _____ of glass.

4. Their spaceship _____
   several tons.

5. Many reporters will _____
   about this trip.

6. There is _____ more test
   to make.

7. The control tower gives the message

   _____ them to begin.

8. They hope to _____
   information that will help people
   on Earth.

1. ___ ___ ___ ___

2. ___ ___ ___ ___

3. ___ ___ ___

4. ___ ___ ___ ___ ___ ___

5. ___ ___ ___ ___

6. ___ ___ ___

7. ___ ___ ___

8. ___ ___ ___ ___

Read down on the spaceship.
What are the astronauts going to do now? _____

Ask and Answer

This is a game to play with a friend.
Use small pieces of paper to make six sets of word cards like these.

| rain | reign |

| brakes | breaks | | cent | scent | | main | mane |

| pail | pale |

| steal | steel |

Each player gets one card from each set.
Take turns.
Close your eyes and put a finger on the game board.
Read the question you are pointing to.
If you have the right word to answer the question, tape the word card over the question on the board.
If you point to a question that is already answered, take another turn.
Keep playing until all the questions are answered.

How might a frightened person look?	What do you use to stop a car?	What is another name for a penny?
What is the period during which a queen or king rules?	What does a thief do?	What is the largest or most important street in a town?
What do we call the smell of a flower?	What is a round container for carrying water?	What happens to a glass that falls to the floor?
What is the long hair on the back of a lion called?	What falls from the clouds during a storm?	What material is used to build the frame of a tall building?

5 Riddles

A riddle is a question with a tricky answer.
Read each riddle below.
Choose one of the words under the blank to complete the answer.
Write the word you choose on the blank.
Compare your completed riddles with your classmates.
Discuss how each answer is tricky.

1. If you put several ducks in a box, what do you have?

   A box of _____.
           crackers   quackers

2. How did the rocket lose its job?

   It was _____.
         fired   tired

3. What is a good way to keep a dog off the street?

   Put it in a _____ lot.
       parking   barking

4. Why can't I make a phone call to the zoo?

   The _____ are busy.
       lines   lions

5. Would you like some more alphabet soup?

   No, I can't eat another _____.
       syllable   spoonful

6. What is a mosquito's favorite sport?

   Skin _____.
       diving   driving

7. Why is tennis such a noisy game?

   Each player raises a _____.
       rattle   racket

8. What animals need to be oiled?

   Mice, because they _____.
       squeak   speak

9. What is an astronaut sandwich made of?

   _____ meat.
     Lunch   Launch

What Does It Mean?

Do this activity with an adult.
Read what the scientists are saying in each cartoon picture.
Work together.
Decide what you think the word in dark print means.
Write the meaning of the word below the picture.

6 ⟩ Color Your Sentences

A colorful description compares two things in an unusual way.
For each box, read the sentence beginnings on the left.
Then read the sentence endings on the right.
Draw a line from the beginning of each sentence to the
ending that makes the best colorful description.

Her eyes were   as heavy as rocks.

The kangaroo jumped   as big as pizzas.

The boxes were   as high as the stars.

The thirsty boy   looks like diamonds.

The motor   sounds like a hive of bees.

The light on the water   drank like a fish.

The ticking clock is   a time bomb.

The little puppy is   an oven.

This room is   a real clown.

Look around your classroom or your home.

Find something that is *as red as a beet.* _____

Think of something that is *a walking encyclopedia.* _____

Look for something that *walks like an elephant.* _____

Now use your imagination to complete these sentences.

_____ as loud as thunder.

_____ is a grumpy old bear.

_____ like a shooting star.

Completing similes and metaphors   **213**

What's It Like?

This is a game for two players.
Make ten word cards like these.

spider	earthquake	ice cube	trumpet	microphone
moon	dream	marshmallow	rainbow	chimpanzee

Put the cards face down.
Take turns.
Select one card.
Read the word on the card to yourself.
Then describe the object on the card by answering each
question on the Question Board.
Try to use colorful descriptions.
If the other player guesses what the object is, keep the card.
If the player does not guess the object, return the card face down.
Play until there are no more words left to describe.

Question Board

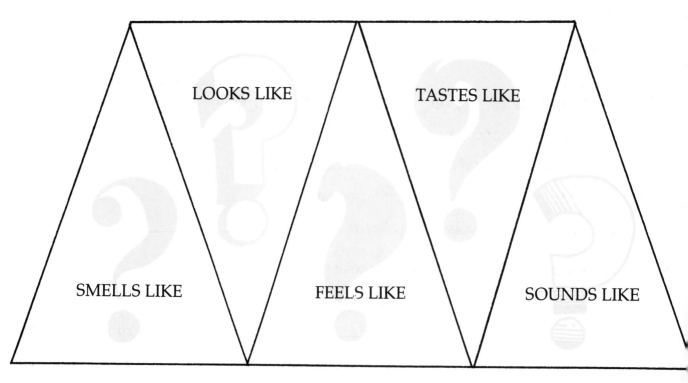

LOOKS LIKE   TASTES LIKE

SMELLS LIKE   FEELS LIKE   SOUNDS LIKE

7 > Crosswords

Read each clue.
Decide what word completes the sentence and fits in the crossword puzzle.
Write the answer in the puzzle.

ACROSS

1. *Finger* is to _____ as *toe* is to *foot*.

4. _____ is to *out* as *up* is to *down*.

7. *Shoes* are to *feet* as _____ are to *hands*.

9. *Snow* is to *cold* as _____ is to *hot*.

10. *Minute* is to *hour* as *day* is to _____.

11. *Water* is to _____ as *air* is to *airplane*.

13. *Brother* is to *boy* as _____ is to *girl*.

15. *Easy* is to _____ as *hard* is to *difficult*.

DOWN

2. *Library* is to *books* as *cupboard* is to _____.

3. _____ is to *bed* as *sit* is to *chair*.

5. *Brake* is to *stop* as _____ is to *go*.

6. *Fruit* is to *apple* as *vegetable* is to _____.

8. *Dog* is to _____ as *bird* is to *chirps*.

9. *Broom* is to _____ as *pen* is to *write*.

10. *Penny* is to *dollar* as *foot* is to _____.

12. _____ is to *skate* as *water* is to *swim*.

14. *One* is to _____ as *three* is to *four*.

Ladder Climb

Play this game with an adult.
Use long narrow strips of paper to make twelve word cards like these.

| breakfast |

| brush | | hear | | clean | | time | | sing |

| write | | country | | insect | | king | | fins |

| shape |

Turn the cards face down.
Choose a card. Read the word on it.
If the word on the card answers one of the questions on your ladder, tape the card below the question.
If you cannot use the card, turn it back over.
Take turns.
The first player to complete a ladder wins the game.

Player 1

If eyes look, what do ears do?

If a robin is a bird, what is a beetle?

If you read a story, what do you do with a song?

If you comb your hair, what do you do to your teeth?

If a princess may become queen, what might a prince become?

If mud makes you dirty, what does soap make you?

Player 2

If a dog has paws, what does a fish have?

If a calendar tells the date, what does a clock tell?

If you draw with a crayon, what do you do with a pencil?

If blue is a color, what is a circle?

If you eat dinner in the evening, what do you eat in the morning?

If Ohio is a state, what is the United States?

Wagon Wheels

Read the group of words on each wheel.
In the center, write a name for the group.

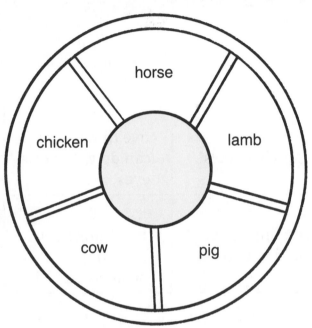

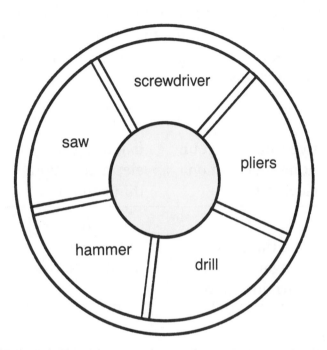

Read the group name in the center of the first wheel.
Complete the wheel with words that belong in the group.
Then do the second wheel.
Fill in the name of a group and five words that belong in it.

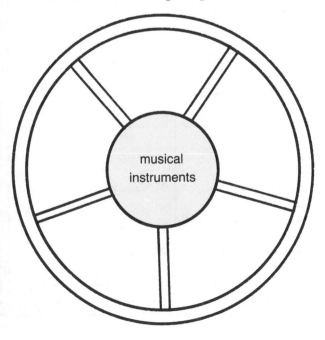

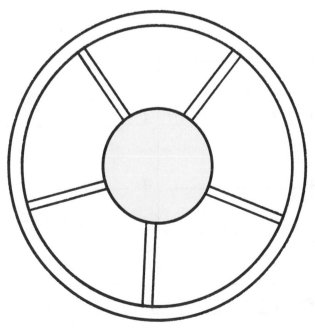

List Five

This is an activity for you to do with a friend or family member.
Work together.
Choose four boxes and write the box numbers on the chart below.
Then complete the chart by listing the things asked for in the boxes.
Try to list the most unusual things you can think of.
Take your chart to school tomorrow and compare your lists
with your classmates' lists.

1 five things in your home that run on electricity	2 five things an elephant might think about	3 five ways a snowball feels	4 five things you can do with your eyes
5 five things a kangaroo could learn in school	6 five ways a rainbow looks	7 five things a robot would like to eat	8 five things you can do with a skateboard

Box _____

1. _____

2. _____

3. _____

4. _____

5. _____

Box _____

1. _____

2. _____

3. _____

4. _____

5. _____

Box _____

1. _____

2. _____

3. _____

4. _____

5. _____

Box _____

1. _____

2. _____

3. _____

4. _____

5. _____

9 Monster Poem

Read the word that goes down the side of the page.
What other words does it make you think of?
Write three words on the blanks after each letter.
The words must begin with the letter at the beginning of the row.
When you are finished, you will have a funny word poem.
Practice reading your poem to yourself.
Write a title for your poem on the line above it.
Then read your poem out loud to your friends, classmates,
and family.

_____

M *merry* _____ _____

O _____ _____ _____

N _____ _____ _____

S _____ _____ _____

T _____ _____ _____

E _____ _____ _____

R _____ _____ _____

Try writing another poem on a separate piece of paper.
Write your name or a favorite word down the side.
Then complete the poem as you did above.

One Word Leads to Another

Do this activity with an adult.
What words does each picture make you think of?
Follow the arrows and take turns adding words.
Continue until all the blanks around each picture are filled.
Then read the words around each picture to a friend or
family member.
See if he or she can guess what the picture is.

start

around

start

10 How Many?

Read each word.
Color all one syllable words orange.
Color all two syllable words yellow.
Color all three syllable words green.
Color all four syllable words blue.
Color all five syllable words red.

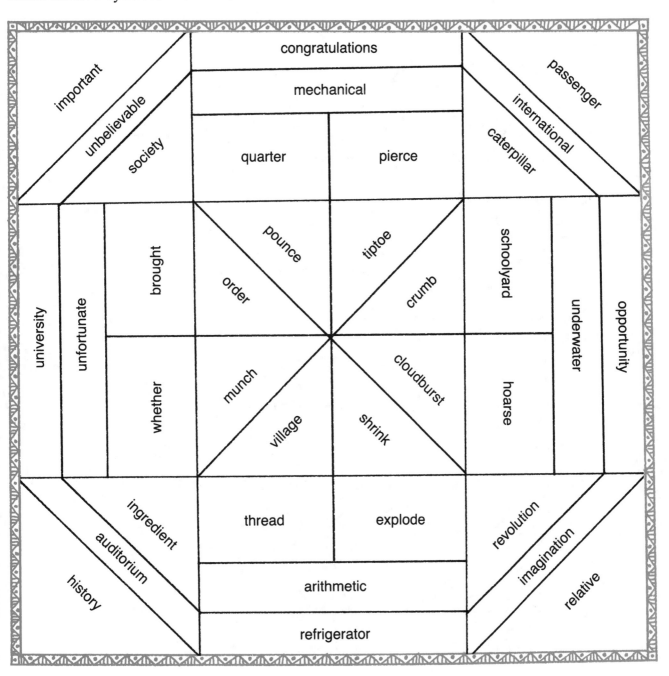

Syllable Sprint

Ask someone to play this game with you.
Make two small markers to use on the game board.
Write each player's name on a marker.
Take turns. Flip a coin on each turn.
Move your marker ahead two spaces for heads.
Move ahead one space for tails.
Read the word on which you land and count the number of syllables.
Move ahead one space for each syllable.
The first player to reach the finish line is the winner.

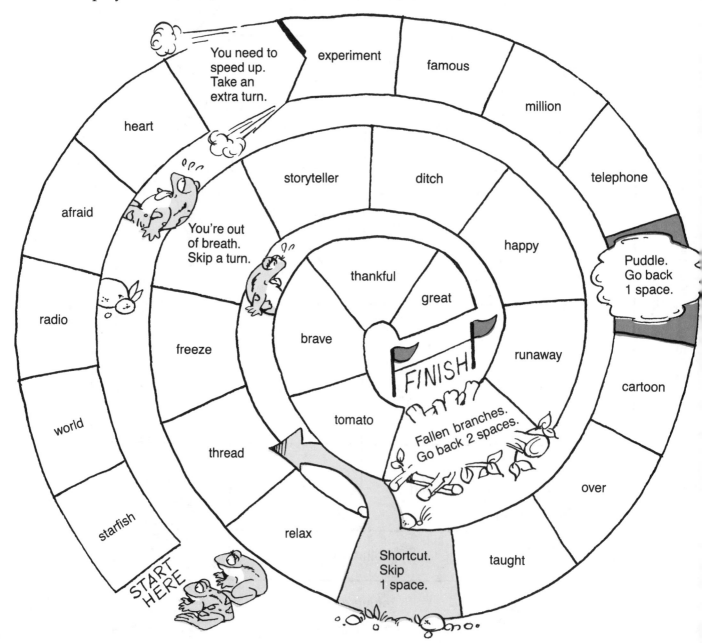

11 ▷ Sentence Scramble

Here are some scrambled sentences.
Unscramble each sentence by putting the
words in alphabetical order.
Write the new sentence on the line.
Then suppose the words in each sentence
are on a dictionary page.
Choose the correct guide words for each
page from the words in the box.
Write the guide words at the beginning
and end of each sentence.

Guide Word Box			
time	wring	curb	and
prove	crew	wrap	two
away	took	part	would
price	am	cave	tear
when	car	pail	aunt

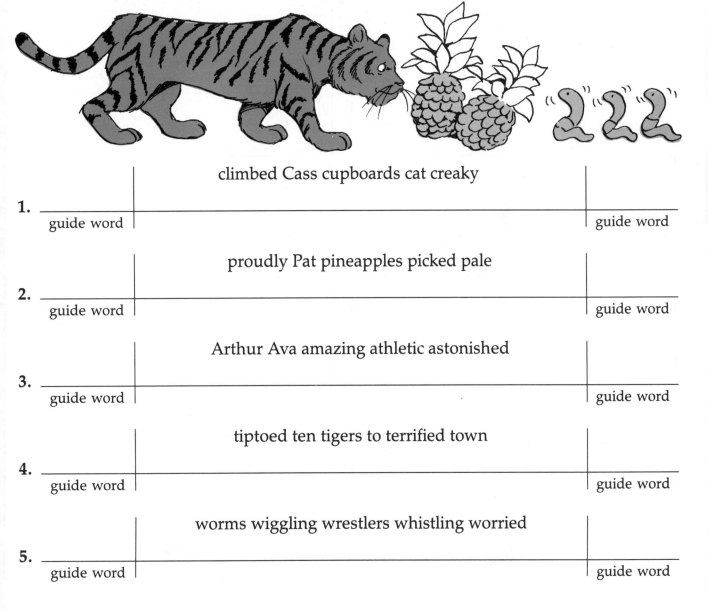

1.   climbed Cass cupboards cat creaky

guide word | | guide word

2.   proudly Pat pineapples picked pale

guide word | | guide word

3.   Arthur Ava amazing athletic astonished

guide word | | guide word

4.   tiptoed ten tigers to terrified town

guide word | | guide word

5.   worms wiggling wrestlers whistling worried

guide word | | guide word

Look Around

Ask someone at home to do this activity with you.
Read the guide words on each dictionary page.
Work together.
Look around your home for objects whose names come
between the guide words on each page.
On each dictionary page, write the names of five objects you find.
Then number the words in alphabetical order.

bank / build

scale / swim

meal / my

fact / fuzz

② Entry Mix-Ups

Look at the dictionary pages below.
The parts of two dictionary entries are mixed up.
Sort out the entries.
Next to each picture, write the correct parts of the entry that
go with the picture.

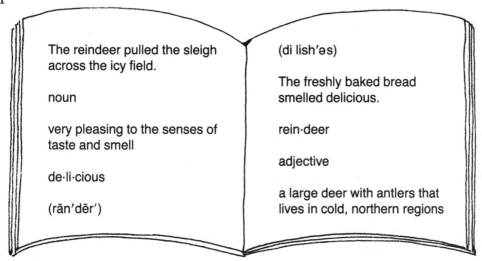

The reindeer pulled the sleigh across the icy field.

noun

very pleasing to the senses of taste and smell

de·li·cious

(rān′dēr′)

(di lish′əs)

The freshly baked bread smelled delicious.

rein·deer

adjective

a large deer with antlers that lives in cold, northern regions

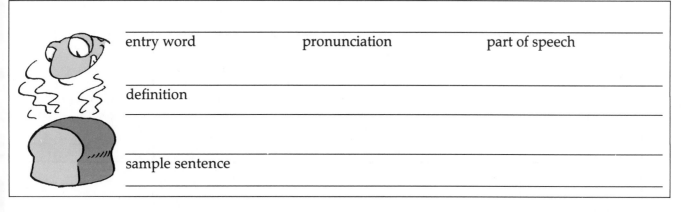

entry word   pronunciation   part of speech

definition

sample sentence

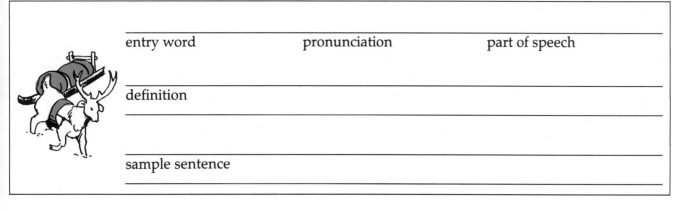

entry word   pronunciation   part of speech

definition

sample sentence

Dictionary Disks

Play this game with a friend.
Make five playing cards like these.
Put the cards in a pile and turn the pile face down.
Take the top card.
Then toss a penny onto the game board.
Read what is written on the computer disk your penny lands on.
If what is written on the disk is an example of the part of a dictionary entry named on your card, score 5 points.
If you land on BUG or ERROR, lose 2 points.
Then return the card to the bottom of the pile.
Take turns and keep score on a piece of paper.
Play until one player scores more than 15 points.

entry word	pronunciation
part of speech	
definition	sample sentence

mem•o•ry	to feed information into a computer	(kəm pyoo'tər)	ERROR	We developed a program to help forecast the weather.
She put the floppy disk into the computer.	BUG	a gadget used to make choices on a computer screen	da•ta	adjective
a list showing what choices are available in a computer program	in•put	noun	He entered the names of all 50 states.	(kē'bôrd')
verb	(skrēn)	men•u	BUG	the part of a computer that stores information

Haunted House

This is a map of a haunted house.

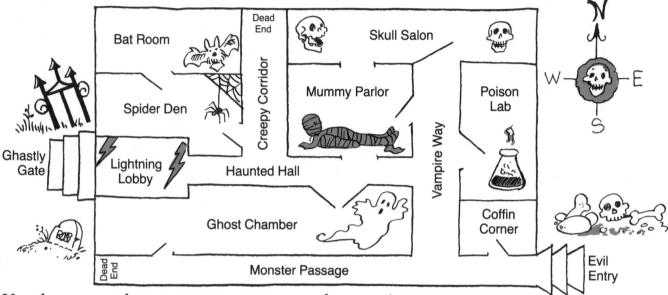

Use the map and map compass to answer the questions.

1. If you are brave enough to enter the house through the Ghastly Gate, what is the first room you come to? _____

2. You walk along the Haunted Hall and then along the Creepy Corridor. What is at the end of the Creepy Corridor? _____

3. You hear strange noises coming from the Bat Room. You want to investigate. Which room do you have to go through to get to the Bat Room? _____

4. You are chased into the Ghost Chamber through the double doors. You escape out the small door to the Monster Passage. If you want to hide in the Coffin Corner, in which direction should you run? _____

5. You have just left the Poison Lab after checking out the equipment. In which direction do you go on Vampire Way to get to the Skull Salon? _____

6. From the Skull Salon you can walk directly into which room? _____

7. After seeing all those mummies in the Mummy Parlor, you have had enough of this haunted house. You go out the door on Vampire Way and run south to the Monster Passage. Then you go east. Through what do you escape? _____

Word Count

Do this activity with an adult.

Choose one page in any book.

Look for these six words which are used most often in books.

a   and   in   of   the   to

Count the number of times you find each word and tally the words below.

Stop when you get to the bottom of the page or when you have counted 20 of one of the words.

Then record your results on the bar graph.

Fill in the spaces above each word to show how many times the word was used.

a	and	in	of	the	to

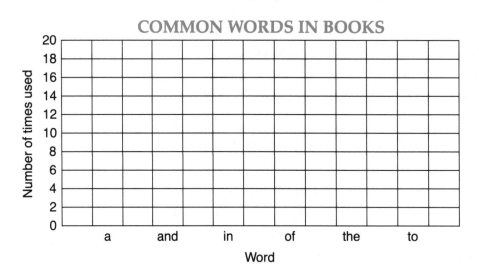

Which word was used most often? _____

Which word was used least often? _____

Do another word count and graph on a separate sheet of paper. Use another book or a different page in the same book.

Was the same word used most often? _____

Was the same word used least often? _____

4 Cross Out

Read each paragraph.
All the sentences but one are about the same idea.
Find the sentence that does not belong and cross it out.

Stephanie Mills was singing almost before she could talk. She would sing with the radio, sing to her family, and sing with her friends. She liked to imagine she was a movie director or an orchestra conductor. Her parents sent her to acting school for professional training, and eventually she got a part in a Broadway show. Stephanie's older sister was also an actress. But Stephanie didn't become a Broadway star until she was 13 and she won the part of Dorothy in a show called *The Wiz*. She played the part for four years, and it was the beginning of her career as a famous singer.

One day in 1956, twelve-year-old Bobby Fischer visited the Manhattan Chess Club. He had never played there before, but he felt sure he could beat even the best players in the room. Once Bobby played on a park bench through a rainstorm. Bobby started to play, and a few people came over to watch. Then more people crowded around to watch Bobby make his moves. These men and women were experienced players, yet they were amazed at how brilliantly Bobby played. Little did they know that two years later Bobby would be the chess champion of the United States.

Reid Rondell trained for more than a year in order to be strong enough for the rough and tumble job of doing stunts. Then, when he was ten, Reid began his career as a stunt person. He does things in movies and TV shows that are too dangerous for the actors to do. Reid also likes to surf and water ski. He practices his stunts over and over so that everything is planned out before the stunt is performed. On screen, it looks like the actors are falling off horses, crashing cars, or jumping off mountains. But in reality, stunt people like Reid are doing these things.

Betty Bennett was just ten years old when she made her first solo airplane flight. Her father sold airplanes and there was an airfield behind her house. She sat in the plane by herself and waited for the engine to warm up. Then she gave the engine more gas, and the plane began to roll forward. It moved slowly at first. Then it raced faster down the runway. Finally the plane lifted into the air like a bird, gliding up into the sky. Betty swooped through the air over blue water. She circled over green fields and forests. When it was time to return, she drifted to the ground in a perfect landing.

What do all the paragraphs above tell about? _____

_____

What's It All About?

Here is an activity for three or more people.
Take turns reading a paragraph aloud.
As a group, discuss what the paragraph is about.
Then decide what the main idea is.
Write the main idea on the lines below the paragraph.

Unlike human workers, robots can work non-stop for long periods. They never get tired, and they always work with the same exactness. They can also work under conditions that humans could not bear, where it is very hot, very noisy, or where there are dangerous rays.

_____

_____

Some small insects live for only a few hours or days. At the other extreme, a tortoise may live for 150 years or more. Some plants, especially trees, live much longer. There are giant sequoia trees in California that began life almost 4000 years ago and some pine trees that are as old as the ancient pyramids.

_____

_____

Franklin Pierce was President from 1853 to 1857. He wanted to take over Hawaii, which was still independent, but nothing came of it. He tried to buy Cuba from Spain, but that only made Spain angry. But he did manage to buy a narrow strip of land from Mexico. Today this forms part of New Mexico and Arizona.

_____

_____

A star lasts many millions of years, but eventually the gases inside it start to break down. This causes great heating, and the star swells up like a balloon, creating a red giant star. Much material is lost to space. Finally the red giant shrinks and becomes a cold, white dwarf star.

_____

_____

Do you like fruits and vegetables? Well, how about digging into a watermelon that weighs 270 pounds? Or an orange the size of a human head? What about a peanut almost four inches long? Or an onion as big as a basketball? People have actually grown these large foods, and most of the foods have won prizes.

_____

_____

Your brain is in charge of everything. It makes sure your body is breathing, hearing, moving, feeling, and performing hundreds more tasks without you even noticing. Even while you are asleep, your brain is on duty, keeping you breathing and making sure all the parts of your body are working together.

_____

_____

Ghost Town

Some modern-day explorers discovered a western ghost town.
They made this chart to show what they discovered.

EXPLORATION OF WEST RANGE JUNCTION

Place Discovered	Dates Explored	Objects Found	Information About Citizens
General Store	September 10–12	herb jars flour sack	Owned by Mr. and Mrs. Bridges
Gold Mine	October 14–17	gold flakes panning equipment mining tools	Operated by G. Lawrence
Jail	October 11–13	sheriff's badge handcuffs	Outlaws killed Sheriff Marks in 1831
Schoolhouse	September 7–8	slate readers	Miss Hastings taught for 25 years

Use the chart to answer the following questions.

1. Which place was explored first? _____

2. Who owned the general store? _____

3. Which places were explored in October? _____

4. What objects were found in the general store? _____

5. Who killed Sheriff Marks? _____

6. In which place were the most objects found? _____

7. Which citizen helped children learn to read? _____

What do you think was the purpose of the exploration?

_____

_____

All About Me

Ask a family member to help you with these activities.

My Numbers
You can describe yourself with numbers.
Choose eight of the items listed below.
Fill in the circle in front of each item you choose.
Then have your family member help you find the numbers.
Write each number after the item.

○ length of nose _____   ○ number of T-shirts _____

○ length of thumb _____   ○ number of pairs of sneakers _____

○ length of little toe _____   ○ how long it takes to count to 100 _____

○ length of hair _____   ○ how long can hold breath _____

○ length of foot _____   ○ how long it takes to brush teeth _____

○ time born _____   ○ how long it takes to say alphabet _____

○ lucky number _____   ○ how far can jump _____

Rectangle or Square?
You can also describe yourself as a shape.
Get a ball of string and a pair of scissors.
Have your family member cut a piece of string equal
to your height.
Then cut a piece as long as your outstretched arms.
Compare the pieces of string.
If one is longer than the other, you are a rectangle.
If they are the same length, you are a square.
Write your name in the rectangle or square to show
which shape you are.

Consider the new things you learned about yourself.
Which three things were most surprising?

Rectangle

Square

_____   _____   _____

If your friends or other family members are interested, help
them find out their numbers and shapes.

6 Time Trip

A newspaper reporter living in the year 2100 took a trip back
in time.
The reporter wrote an article about the trip.
Read the article.
Then complete the items at the end.

THE LOSHAR NEWS

On my last vacation, I decided to take a trip back in time. I went back more than a century and visited the United States in the year 1991.

Of course I saw many strange and unusual things. What surprised me most, though, was how the people entertain themselves. What seems to be their favorite entertainment involves the use of a large box-shaped container. The container either stands on legs or rests on a table or shelf. On one side of the container, the side people look at, is a piece of glass. Nearby, either on the container, a separate panel, or a hand-held pad, are the controls. When you operate the controls, the glass lights up in several colors. Images parade across the glass. Music and speech come forth. People spend hours watching and listening to their container. They laugh at the container, they talk about it, and generally seem to just adore it.

1. Write four important details from the article that describe
   the object or explain how it works.

   _____

   _____

   _____

   _____

2. What object or activity is the reporter writing about?

   _____

3. Write a headline for the article.

   _____

4. Draw a picture of the object in the space to the right of the article.

Missing Parts

Work together with a friend.
Complete each paragraph by filling in the blanks.
Use the part of speech written below the blank or write a
sentence if it says "sentence."
Be as silly as you like and have fun.
When you are finished, read the paragraphs aloud.

No one had ever seen a talking hamster before, but the _____
                                                              adjective

_____ hamster just _____ and _____ all
        adjective   verb   verb

day long. Only its friend the _____ seemed to care, and it said so
                                    noun

quite _____. "_____
          adverb   sentence

_____," it complained.

Many years ago, a very timid dragon lost its way in a(n) _____. First
                                                                noun

it _____, but that didn't help at all. So the dragon _____
        verb   verb

and _____ to try to scare away the huge _____ in the
        verb   noun

nearby _____. But when the people saw the _____
            noun   adjective

_____ dragon coming, all they could say was, "_____!"
    adjective   interjection

This is the tale of a(n) _____ who _____ whenever it
                            noun   verb

_____ a(n) _____. Now most people had never seen
        verb   noun

a(n) _____ _____, so no one paid any attention when
        adjective   noun

a(n) _____ _____ _____ onto the road.
        noun   verb   adverb

Finally it _____ _____ and _____ the
              verb   adverb   verb

_____ _____.
    adjective   noun

7 Story Match

Read the story on the left and find the sentence on the right that tells what happened next.
Use a ruler to connect the dots between the parts that go together.

Rosa put on her sweat suit and running shoes. She jumped and stretched to warm up. Rosa was in good shape today.

•   W

N   A   R

•   It sailed high into the sky.

Oscar put a worm on a hook and dropped his fishing line into the water. The hook floated down. Soon Oscar felt a tug on the line.

•   P   L

T

•   He had caught a giant fish.

Jill helped Leah get her kite in the air. For a while the kite moved with the wind. Then Leah tripped and let go of the kite.

L

•   E

R   B

M

•   He was sold out in less than an hour.

Agnes strummed her guitar. She tightened a string and then plucked it. Finally Agnes broke into song.

E   A

•   W

S

•   She jogged more than two miles.

Ray fixed up his old bicycle. He cleaned and polished the frame and filled the tires with air. Then he set off down the road.

D

L   U

•   I   O

•   A large group gathered to listen.

It was the hottest day so far this year. Kenzo decided to make a pitcher of lemonade. Then he set up a table at the roadside and put up a big sign.

B

C

•   N

•   He went racing toward the lake.

Circle all the letters not covered by a line.
Write the circled letters in order from top to bottom.

They spell the name of a delicious treat. _____

Round Robin

Do this activity with one or more friends.
Read the story beginnings below.
Choose the one you like best and circle it.
Read your choice aloud.
Then take turns adding a sentence to the story.
Keeping passing the story around until it is finished.
Each person may have several turns.
Continue on a separate sheet of paper if you need more room.
Read the story aloud when you are finished.

Princess Lella stood at the entrance to the cave. She gripped the magic sword more tightly. It seemed to grow hot in her hand.

"OK," José said as he pulled back the curtain. "This is it." Behind the curtain was the most wonderful contraption we had ever seen.

"Hey, cut that out," shouted a big, booming voice.
"What was that?" asked Murel.
"I'm the tree you just hit with your ax," came the reply.
"And I'm in no mood to be tickled."

We had heard about a giant creature that roamed the woods, but we didn't believe it really existed. Yet here we were, staring down at these *gigantic* footprints.

_____

_____

_____

_____

_____

_____

_____

Where Does It Go?

Read the title and author of each book.
Decide in which bookcase the book belongs.
Write the title of the book on a shelf in the bookcase.

A TRIP to the ZOO by Ann Immel

The Little People by To B. Tiny

Kids in the Kitchen by Watta Mess

SPORTS JOKES & RIDDLES by Make M. Laugh

HOW TO MAKE PIZZA by O. VEN

PLAY BALL! by Doug Out

What SWIMS in the OCEAN? by C. Creature

The LOST PRINCE by Ivan Togohome

Cooking is Fun by U. Bakem

BIRDWATCHER'S HANDBOOK by Burdon Thehand

Soccer for Everyone by Yul Kickim

Telephone Twins by Wee Callyou

Cooking	Animals	Sports	People

Which bookcase contains books most interesting to you? _____

Which book in that bookcase would you most like to read? _____

Story Sense

This is a game to play with an adult.
Copy the sentences below on a piece of paper.
Write each sentence on a separate line and leave space between the lines.
Cut between the sentences so that you have twelve sentence strips.
Mix up the strips.
Place them face up and end-to-end in two rows, one below the other.
Now take turns.
Change the position of any two sentence strips.
Read the story aloud from beginning to end.
If the story makes sense, you win.
If the story does not make sense, keep playing until it does.

I got up very early the next day.

I built a huge snowhouse.

It was very warm inside.

The ground was covered with snow.

I put on my warm winter clothes.

The weather report said it had also gotten warm outside.

All day long I played in my snowhouse.

I ran to look out the window.

My snowhouse had melted to the ground!

I got washed and took off my pajamas.

I ran out into the snow.

I woke up and looked out my window.

Consider the Facts

What can you figure out from each set of facts?
Circle the letter of the choice you think is most likely true.
When you are finished, compare your answers with your classmates.
Discuss why you chose each answer.

Fact Set 1

A girl lost her baseball.
She threw it so hard it went over the fence.

a. The ball was actually a softball.
b. The ball was caught on the other side of the fence.
c. The ball could not be more than a mile away.

Fact Set 2

There was a sudden rainstorm.
There are footprints in the kitchen.

a. Someone was wearing new shoes.
b. Someone walked through the mud.
c. Someone was caught without an umbrella.

Fact Set 3

It is twelve noon.
The front door of the building is locked.

a. There is no one in the building.
b. There is an open door in the back.
c. There is no school on Saturday.

Fact Set 4

There is a clock on the wall.
Its hands are not moving.

a. The clock will show the same time in five minutes.
b. The clock is missing some parts.
c. The clock fell off the wall the day before.

Fact Set 5

An animal escaped from the zoo.
It squeezed through bars that were two feet apart.

a. The animal escaped at night.
b. The animal was a black seal.
c. The animal was not an elephant.

Fact Set 6

Two lamps were turned on.
The room was still quite dark.

a. The lamps were very old.
b. The light bulbs had burned out.
c. The lamp shades were dark blue.

Making inferences   **239**

Guess Where

Ask a friend to help you take this challenge.
Do not read below the dotted line.
Have your friend read each list to you one sentence at a time.
After you hear each sentence, take one guess at where you are.
Have your friend tell you if you are right or wrong.
If you guessed wrong, go on to the next sentence.
If you guessed right, score 10 points minus 1 point for each sentence that was read to you.
Compute your score in the score box.
Try for a grand total of 15 points or more for all three places.

Place 1
1. People are cheering.
2. A horse is galloping around.
3. There are ropes above your head.
4. You can smell popcorn.
5. You are inside a tent.
6. You hear a lion roar.
7. You see acrobats and clowns.   ANSWER: CIRCUS

Score Box

10 − [ ] = [ ]
              TOTAL

Place 2
1. Many people are wearing matching clothes.
2. Someone is throwing something.
3. People keep looking up in the air.
4. Some people are pushing each other.
5. Someone in a striped shirt is blowing a whistle.
6. There are tall metal posts nearby.
7. Someone is yelling, "Hike!"   ANSWER: FOOTBALL GAME

Score Box

10 − [ ] = [ ]
              TOTAL

Place 3
1. A loud alarm is ringing.
2. People are rushing to get dressed.
3. The people are putting on coats, gloves, and boots.
4. Some people are putting on big helmets.
5. People are sliding down a pole.
6. Several large trucks are nearby.
7. The trucks are carrying ladders, hoses, and axes.

ANSWER: FIRE STATION

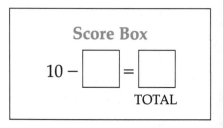

Score Box

10 − [ ] = [ ]
              TOTAL

GRAND TOTAL _____

Headlines

Read each newspaper headline.
Circle the statement that gives the probable reason for
the headline.

• The Record •
★ EXTRA ★

GIANT WAVES STRIKE COAST

earthquake in Colorado

tornado across Kansas

hurricane near Florida

• The NEWS •

Famous Actress Gone!

movie star changed name

new movie closed

movie star disappeared

THE GAZETTE

**TONS OF SNOW
ALL ROADS CLOSED**

snow shovelers strike

sudden winter storm

new highway construction

∼ The Advance ∼

New Crater Discovered on Moon

scientists using powerful new
telescopes

astronauts training for space
mission

pilots flying world's fastest
airplane

Write a reason for this headline on
the newspaper.

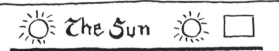

The Sun

Dallas Knee-Deep in Sheep

explosion in sweater factory

escaped farm animals

people wearing shorts

⊙ Our Town News ⚑ ⊙

"Noise Must Stop!" says Mayor

What Happened?

Play this game with someone in your family.
Cut out sixteen pieces of paper the size of the boxes below.
Place one piece of paper over each box.
Take turns.
Uncover one Cause box and one Effect box.
Read the cause and effect aloud.
If the cause and effect go together, leave the boxes uncovered and score 2 points.
If the cause and effect do not match, recover the boxes.
Keep score on a piece of paper.
The first player to score 10 points is the winner.

Cause

The waiter spilled tomato soup on me.	We mixed yellow and blue paint together.
Yoko pulled on the oars.	Stan blew into his trumpet.
Kerri plugged the cord into the wall.	Jake lost his eyeglasses.
The baby knocked over a glass of water.	A cold wind was blowing.

Effect

Colored lights lit up the room.	We heard a loud blast of sound.
There is a puddle on the floor.	He kept bumping into things.
We put on our warm coats.	There are red stains on my shirt.
We painted our doghouse green.	The boat glided through the water.

21 ▸ Who Did It?

Someone has robbed a bank.
Can you figure out who did it?
The signs the people are holding will give you clues.
After you read each clue, write the first letter of the clue on
the line at the bottom of the page.
Then do what the clue says.
Start by looking for the person who is not afraid of wild animals.

OUT OF LUCK. I DON'T HAVE TIME TO ROB BANKS. LOOK FOR THE PERSON WHO SAYS BALL GAMES ARE THE BEST SHOWS ON TV.

WHAT? I'M NOT THE PERSON YOU WANT. WHY DON'T YOU LOOK FOR THE PERSON WHO THINKS SUPERMARKETS ARE INTERESTING PLACES TO VISIT?

BANKS? I NEVER ROB THEM! TRY LOOKING FOR THE PERSON WHO SPENDS LOTS OF MONEY IN PAINT STORES.

WHY ASK ME? I'M NOT GUILTY. LOOK FOR THE PERSON WHO FEELS AT HOME ON THE RANGE.

YOU SOLVED THE CRIME! JUST READ THE SENTENCE AT THE BOTTOM OF THE PAGE TO FIND OUT WHO ROBBED THE BANK.

I DON'T WANT TO TALK ABOUT IT! LOOK FOR THE PERSON WHO IS ALWAYS TALKING ABOUT VEGETABLES.

OH, NO! I DIDN'T DO IT. YOU SHOULD LOOK FOR THE PERSON WHO IS REALLY GOOD AT SOLVING CRIMES.

COMPLETELY INNOCENT. MAYBE YOU SHOULD LOOK FOR THE PERSON WHO MOVES IN TIME WITH MUSIC.

The _____ did it.

What a Character!

Work with a friend or an adult.
Read each question.
Answer with the name of a person from books you have read.
You may both give the same answer or different answers.
Choose the left side or right side of the page.
Take turns writing your answers.

1. Who is the funniest person you have ever read about?

   _____   _____

2. Who is the meanest, most rotten person you have read about?

   _____   _____

3. If you had to spend a year on a deserted island with just
   one person, who would it be?

   _____   _____

4. Who is the biggest and strongest person you have read about?

   _____   _____

5. Who would you have a lot of trouble keeping quiet in a library?

   _____   _____

6. Which person reminds you a lot of yourself?

   _____   _____

7. If you could interview anyone on your list, who would it be?

   _____   _____

8. Write three questions you would ask that person.

   _____   _____

   _____   _____

   _____   _____

22 ▶ Picture This

Words can be used to create images, or pictures, in your mind.
Several items are named below.
Picture each item in your mind.
Then circle the letter of the choice that does *not* help you
create an image of the item.

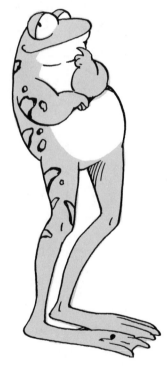

1. an underground cave

   b. darkness
   c. mist
   d. cobwebs
   e. wrinkles

2. a crowded beach

   m. sand castles
   n. falling leaves
   o. colored towels
   p. plastic shovels

3. a car factory

   e. assembly lines
   f. glowing hot metal
   g. palm trees
   h. wheels and doors

4. a jungle

   i. long icicles
   j. warm rain
   k. hanging vines
   l. swarming bugs

5. a library

   l. quiet people
   m. shelves and tables
   n. tennis balls
   o. daily newspapers

6. a carnival

   d. funny performers
   e. frozen dinners
   f. flashing lights
   g. colorful balloons

7. a garbage dump

   b. old papers
   c. noisy trucks
   d. tin cans
   e. new shoes

8. an apple orchard

   q. crisp fruit
   r. clean windows
   s. rows of trees
   t. overloaded baskets

9. a rock band

   s. typewriters
   t. crazy dancing
   u. microphones
   v. loud singing

Can you picture a funny answer to this question?
Write the letters of your choices in order and
"see" what you get.

Q How do trains hear?

A They use their _____.

Mind Reader

Here is an activity for you and a friend.
Take turns.
Choose one item from the item box.
On separate paper, list ten words or phrases that would help
you create an image of the item.
Do not show your list to your friend.
Now tell your friend the name of the item.
Have your friend make his or her own list of ten words or phrases.
Compare your lists.
Score 1 point for each word or phrase that is on both lists.
Record your score below.
Do the activity for six different items.

Item Box		
popcorn	ocean	garden
submarine	lamb	blizzard
old shoes	marching band	motorcycle
telephone	burning building	scarecrow

Item 1	
Item 2	
Item 3	
Item 4	
Item 5	
Item 6	
TOTAL SCORE	

Check How You Did

If your total score is

9 points or less, you could do better.

10–21 points, you are getting warmer.

22–35 points, you are tuned in.

36 points or more, you are mind readers!

23 ▸ What Four?

Read each question.
Write your answers on the lines.
When you are finished, compare your answers with
your classmates.

1. If you dug straight down from the ground, what four
   things would you probably find?

   _____   _____

   _____   _____

2. If you went to the doctor because you felt very hot, what
   four things would the doctor probably do?

   _____   _____

   _____   _____

3. If you were to spend a week on a deserted island, what
   four things would you need to bring along?

   _____   _____

   _____   _____

4. If you visited a museum, what four different things might
   be on display?

   _____   _____

   _____   _____

5. If you were to be a teacher for one day, what four things
   would you need in class?

   _____   _____

   _____   _____

Strange Situations

Ask a friend to do this activity with you.
Four strange situations are given below.
Read each question.
Work together to decide on your answers.
Write your answers on the lines.

1. If you could build a farm on the moon, what three things would it have that most other farms have?

   what three things would it have that *no* other farm has?

   _____
   _____
   _____

2. If you were only three inches tall, what three new things would you be able to do?

   what three things would you *not* be able to do?

   _____
   _____
   _____

3. If you could train an elephant to compete in the Olympics, which two events would it probably win?

   in which two events would it come in last?

   _____
   _____

4. If it snowed on the 4th of July, what two things would you be unable to do?

   what two things could you do for the first time ever?

   _____
   _____

Now work together to make a poster for one of the situations.
Include pictures showing your answers to the questions.
Take your poster to school tomorrow and show it to your classmates.

Follow the Plan

The plan below will help you write a story.
Choose one or more characters from the character box, or make up your own characters.
Name the characters and write their names on the line provided.
Next choose a place from the place box, or use a place you like better.
Write the name of the place on the first line of "Setting."
Now think about what will happen in your story.
Fill in the rest of the story plan with your ideas.

Character	
firefighter	ghost
robot	ballplayer
dragon	singer

Place	
volcano	fireworks show
Africa	movie studio
toy store	sunken ship

1. **Characters** _____

2. **Setting**   Where the story takes place _____

   When the story takes place _____

3. **Problem**   What needs to be worked out _____

   _____

4. **Goal**   What the characters want to accomplish _____

   _____

5. **Action**   Events in the story _____

   _____

   _____

   Reactions to the events _____

   _____

6. **Outcome**   Results of the events and reactions _____

   _____

Now write a story based on your story plan.
Write your story on separate paper.
When you are finished, share your story with your classmates.

Story Map

Do this activity with an adult.
Get a copy of one of your favorite stories.
If the story is short, read the entire story for this activity.
If the story is long, use just one or two chapters.
Write the title and author on the line below.
Then take turns reading the story aloud page-by-page.
After a page is read, fill in whatever you can on the story map.
Use the completed map to retell the story in your own words.

Story map for _____ by _____.

Characters

Setting (time, place)

Problem (what needs to be worked out)

Goal (what characters want to accomplish)

Action (events, reactions)

Outcome (results of Action)

Know Your Planets

A fact is something that can be counted, checked, or tested.
An opinion is what someone thinks or feels about something.
Read each statement.
Circle **F** for *fact* or **O** for *opinion*.

1. Neptune rotates once every 18 to 20 hours.   **F   O**

2. Venus is named for the Roman goddess of love and beauty.   **F   O**

3. The planets are the most beautiful objects in the sky.   **F   O**

4. Mars is sometimes called the Red Planet.   **F   O**

5. A day on Mercury is equal to 59 days on Earth.   **F   O**

6. The planets do not produce their own heat and light.   **F   O**

7. Uranus is not a very interesting planet.   **F   O**

8. Visitors from Mars have probably landed on Earth.   **F   O**

9. Saturn is surrounded by thousands of rings formed of ice.   **F   O**

10. Pluto is the smallest of all the planets.   **F   O**

11. Looking at the planets through a telescope is fun.   **F   O**

12. One of Jupiter's moons has erupting volcanoes.   **F   O**

13. Everybody ought to know the names of the planets.   **F   O**

14. The atmosphere of Venus is filled with thick clouds.   **F   O**

What do you know about Earth?
Write three facts.

_____

_____

_____

Now write three opinions you have about Earth.

_____

_____

_____

Money, Money

Ask someone to play this game with you.
Take turns.
Choose one statement below and read it aloud.
Decide whether it is a fact or an opinion.
Then use a nickel to check if you are right.
Put the nickel on the shape in the box.
If it completely covers the shape, the statement is a fact.
If some part of the shape shows, the statement is an opinion.
Keep track of how many times you are right.
Do not reuse any boxes.
The first player to be right six times is the winner.

Abraham Lincoln is on the penny.	75¢ is a lot of money.	$1 bills wear out in about 18 months.	All coins contain some copper.
The $2 bill has a nice picture on the back.	A half dollar is worth more than a quarter.	Pennies are the best coins.	It is a good idea to save money.
A quarter has ridges around the edge.	Coin collecting is an interesting hobby.	Paper money is easier to use than coins.	A nickel is bigger than a dime.
A dollar is worth 100 cents.	Paper money is printed on special paper.	A coin is dated with the year it was made.	The United States should use only coins.

26 ▸ Who Wrote It?

People who write ads want you to buy or do something.
They use special ways of writing to convince you.
Look at the pictures below.
Each person works for a different company.
Read what each person is saying.

WE ALWAYS LIKE TO MENTION A FAMOUS PERSON IN OUR ADS.

THE ADS WE CREATE GIVE THE IMPRESSION THAT EVERYBODY HAS THE PRODUCT.

IN OUR ADS WE REPEAT THE NAME OF THE PRODUCT SEVERAL TIMES.

FOR OUR ADS, WE USE THE WORDS OF SOMEONE WHO HAS THE PRODUCT.

Creative Copy
Company

Sell Well
Productions

Ads
Unlimited

Words That
Work, Inc.

Now read each advertisement.
Find the person who describes the way the ad was written.
Write the name of the person's company on the line below the ad.

My soggy breakfast cereal was getting me down. Same old mush every morning. Then I tried new Crisp O's, and my mornings came alive. Each delicious little piece stays crispy and crunchy until I gobble it up. So if you're like me and tired of mush in the morning, try new Crisp O's. You'll be glad you did.

_____

What is everyone talking about these days? What is everyone buying? Our new Song Saver Super System! Best way to organize your records and cassettes. These systems are selling quickly. Don't *you* be left out. Get yours today!

_____

Need a new hair style? Want to look like a movie star? Come to Snip and Clip, the only choice for the best and latest in hair styles. Curly Locks, well-known movie and TV star, never looks better than after a trip to our shop. So visit Snip and Clip soon for hair like the stars.

_____

Hopping Hitops. The only sneakers you'll need. Hopping Hitops. You'll jump higher. You'll run faster. Hopping Hitops put bounce and spring in your step. Hopping Hitops. Get a pair soon and hop, hop, away.

_____

Advertise!

Do this activity with a friend.
The names of some products are given in the box.
Choose one for which you would like to write an ad, or make up your own product.
Work together to make notes for your ad.
Fill in the note card below.

Invisible Ink	Spaghetti Hook
Music Computer	Shadow Saver
Auto Skates	Bubble Chamber
Truth Machine	Crayon Melter

NOTES FOR ADVERTISEMENT

Product Name

Ways to Write About Product

1. Suggest Everybody Has Product

2. Repeat Product Name

3. Name Famous Person

4. Use Words of Person Who Has Product

Now work together to write your advertisement.
Use one or more of the ideas you wrote on the note card.
Work on separate paper until you get your ad just right.
Then write the final ad here.
You may also draw a picture of the product and attach it to the ad.
Take your ad to school tomorrow and read it to your classmates.

Science Search

Read each sentence.
Search for the missing word in the puzzle.
Look across, down, and on a slant.
Circle the word and write it in the sentence.

1. Polar bears live on the floating ice of

   _____ regions.

2. When a _____ erupts,
   blazing lava pours down its slopes.

3. Your _____ is a frame of
   bones that gives your body its shape.

4. In 1969, the first astronauts walked

   on the _____.

5. A _____ is the stony
   remains of an ancient animal.

6. Scientists study the clouds to forecast

   the _____.

7. The _____ over the lake
   kept us from seeing the other shore.

8. _____ is a way of sending
   sounds through space.

9. The rocket shot a _____
   into orbit around the earth.

10. Light forms an image on the inner

    surface of your _____.

11. A grasshopper is an _____
    with strong legs for jumping.

s	a	t	e	l	l	i	t	e
k	v	o	l	c	a	n	o	f
e	a	r	l	b	r	s	e	o
l	m	r	a	t	c	e	f	s
e	e	o	i	d	t	c	o	s
t	y	n	o	s	i	t	g	i
o	t	e	e	n	c	o	i	l
n	n	w	e	a	t	h	e	r

Write the leftover letters from the puzzle.
Go in order across each row from top to bottom.
They spell the name of a famous scientist.

___ ___ ___ ___ ___ ___   ___ ___ ___ ___ ___ ___ ___

Famous Leaders

This is a game for two players.
Take turns.
Close your eyes and put a finger on the game board.
Read what the person you are pointing to is saying.
Then try to discover where the person lived.
The name of the place is hidden in what the person is saying.
The person's home will be one of the places given below.
If you find the name of the place, circle it in the person's speech.
If you point to a person whose home has already been found, take another turn.
Play until all the people's homes have been found.

| China | Germany | Greece | India | Rome | USA |

I ruled all of Europe, from east to west.

Augustus Caesar

The great wall that surrounds my country has not changed much in a thousand years.

Confucius

I led my country in a revolution that made us an independent country.

George Washington

I did not worry if it would anger many people when I helped make my country rich and powerful.

William II

With peace in mind I aided my country's struggle for independence.

Mahatma Gandhi

I thought my form of government was best. Thomas Jefferson seemed to agree, centuries later. He made his country a democracy, also.

Pericles

28 ▶ The Story of ?

A biography is the written story of a person's life.
Answer the questions below.
They will help you get started on a biography of an
imaginary person.

1. What is your imaginary person's name?

   _____

2. When was the person born?

   _____

3. Where does the person live?

   _____

4. What does the person look like?

   _____

5. What are the person's favorite foods?

   _____

6. What are the names of the person's best friends?

   _____

7. What does the person do during the day?

   _____

8. What are the names of the people in the person's family?

   _____

Now that you know some things about
your imaginary person, write a story
about a funny day in the person's life.
Write your story on separate paper.
Then draw a picture of your person in
the picture frame.
Share your story and picture with your
classmates.

My Time Line

Ask an adult in your home to help you with this activity.
Answer each question below about yourself.
Then draw an arrow to the time line to show your age when
you did each thing.

Time Line

1. When and where were you born?

    _____ ●————————————→ ▬0 years old

2. When did you get your first tooth?

    _____ ● ▬1 year old

3. When did you start to walk?

    _____ ● ▬2 years old

4. When did you say your first word? What was it?

    _____ ● ▬3 years old

5. When did you start school?

    _____ ● ▬4 years old

    ▬5 years old

6. When did you first read a book by yourself?
    What was it about?

    _____ ● ▬6 years old

7. When did you first make yourself a sandwich?
    What kind was it? ▬7 years old

    _____ ● ▬8 years old

8. When did you first go somewhere by yourself?
    Where did you go? ▬9 years old

    _____ ● ▬10 years old

9. What was the best thing that happened to you? ▬11 years old

    _____ ● ▬12 years old

Now use some of the information above to write a true story
about your life.
Write your story on separate paper.
Then read your story to your family.
Ask if they can add any details you did not remember.
Add these details to your story and make a final copy.

Shape Poems

Here are some unusual poems to read.
The poems are shaped like what they tell about.

Hi, Ho! I'm headed over a high and mighty hilltop.

A fierce tornado is coming towards us. Run, run away!

Read the poems below.
Choose one and rewrite it in the shape of what it tells about.
Use the space to the right of the poems.

Rainbows
Red, green, blue, yellow, indigo.
Color explosion.

I wish I was a feather
Floating, floating in the wind.

A slimy snake
Slithering, sliding, slinking
Through the grass.

Now use your imagination to write your own shape poem.
Choose one of the shapes below, or use your own shape.
What does the shape make you think of?
On separate paper, write a shape poem about what you thought of.

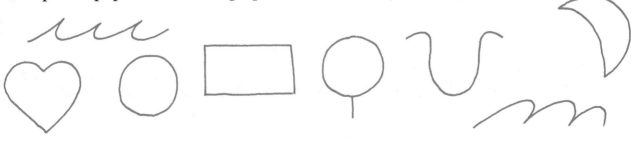

Complete a Poem

Here is an activity for you and a friend.
Start by reading this poem aloud.
It will remind you of what you know about poetry.

> A poem is shorter than a story.
> It tells just one thought at a time.
> The words have a beat when you read them.
> And sometimes the words even rhyme.

Now work together to complete the poem below.
Work on two lines at a time.
The lines may rhyme or not, but try to use the same beat in both lines.
You can count the beats in each line by noticing which syllables are pronounced louder.
When the poem is finished, practice reading it aloud.
Take the poem to school tomorrow and read it to your classmates.

The clock _____

The time for _____

My friend _____

My friend and I _____

We thought we _____

We wished we _____

At last _____

But then _____

My friend and I _____

And now _____

A Golden Tale

A myth is a made-up story about goddesses and gods.
The myth below is from ancient Greece.
Read the myth.
Then answer the questions at the end.

In the land of Lydia there lived a king named Midas. Midas was not a bad king, but he was rather greedy. He had a wife and a daughter who loved him, and a lot of money, but he wanted to be even richer.

One day King Midas did a favor for the god Dionysus. In return, Dionysus told Midas he could make one great wish and it would come true. So the king wished that everything he touched would turn to gold. Dionysus granted the wish and King Midas was overjoyed.

Everything was fine for a short while. The king touched some flowers, and they turned into solid gold blossoms. He touched the branch of a tree, and it turned into a precious golden object.

Then the king had a terrible thought.

"What will happen when I eat?" he wondered. Midas picked up an apple. Before he could bite into it, it turned into gold. "I'll starve," the king wailed. He knew then that he made an awful mistake. He started to sob, and his daughter came to comfort him.

"Stay away!" shouted Midas, but it was too late. When his daughter gave him a hug she was turned into a shiny golden statue.

The king was so full of grief that no one could console him. He begged Dionysus to take away his power. Dionysus heard Midas and granted his wish. Everything changed back to the way it was before, but King Midas was no longer a greedy man. He had learned his lesson.

1. What lesson do you think King Midas learned from this experience?

_____

2. If someone says you "have the Midas touch," what do you think is meant?

_____

3. If you were King Midas, what would you have wished for? Why would you have made this wish?

_____

Chariot Race

Play this game with two friends or family members.
Make three small markers to use on the game board.
Then read about the Greek figures below.
Have each player choose a different one and write the name on a marker.
Take turns. Flip a coin on each turn.
If the coin comes up heads, move ahead one space.
If the coin comes up tails, move ahead two spaces.
The first player to land on FINISH is the winner.

ZEUS was king of all the gods. He lived high in the clouds and ruled the earth and sky. Sometimes he came down to the earth disguised as an animal.
- He commanded the rain and clouds.
- He could throw bolts of lightning.

ATHENA was the goddess of wisdom, bravery, and peace. She ruled over the useful and decorative arts of civilized life. The city of Athens is named for her.
- She wore a helmet, spear, and shield.
- She could tame wild horses.

POSEIDON was the ruler of the sea. He lived in a beautiful palace under the ocean. All the creatures that lived in the water were under his command.
- He controlled the oceans.
- He could cause violent earthquakes.

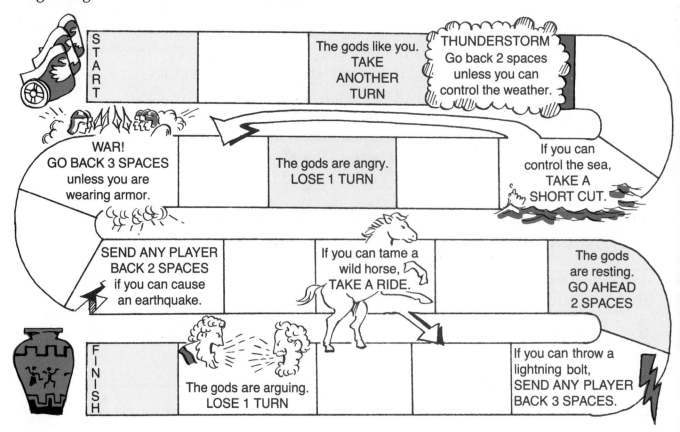

START

The gods like you. TAKE ANOTHER TURN

THUNDERSTORM
Go back 2 spaces unless you can control the weather.

WAR!
GO BACK 3 SPACES unless you are wearing armor.

The gods are angry.
LOSE 1 TURN

If you can control the sea, TAKE A SHORT CUT.

SEND ANY PLAYER BACK 2 SPACES if you can cause an earthquake.

If you can tame a wild horse, TAKE A RIDE.

The gods are resting.
GO AHEAD 2 SPACES

FINISH

The gods are arguing.
LOSE 1 TURN

If you can throw a lightning bolt, SEND ANY PLAYER BACK 3 SPACES.

Enrichment
MATH

Grades 3 & 4
Answer Key and Teaching Suggestions

AMERICAN EDUCATION PUBLISHING

MATH OVERVIEW

ENRICHMENT MATH was developed to provide children with additional opportunities to practice and review mathematical concepts and skills and to use these skills in the home. Children work individually on the first page of each lesson and then with family members on the second page. Every lesson presents high interest activities designed to heighten children's awareness of mathematical ideas and to enrich their understanding of those ideas.

ENRICHMENT MATH consists of 31 two page lessons for grade levels 3 and 4. At each grade level *ENRICHMENT MATH* covers all of the important topics of the traditional mathematics curriculum. Each lesson is filled with games, puzzles and other opportunities for exploring mathematical ideas.

AUTHORS

Peggy Kaye is the author of *Games For Math* and *Games for Reading*. She spent ten years as a classroom teacher in New York City public and private schools, and is today a private tutor in math and reading.

Carole Greenes is Professor of Mathematics at Boston University. She has taught mathematics and mathematics education for more than 20 years and is a former elementary school teacher. Dr. Greenes is the author of a K-8 basal math series and has also written for programs such as *Reach Program, Trivia Math* and the *TOPS-Problem.*

Linda Schulman is Professor of Mathematics at Lesley College . For the past 12 years, she has taught courses in mathematics and mathematics education. Prior to her work at the college level, Dr. Schulman taught elementary school. She is the author of a basal mathematics textbook as well as of other curriculum programs including *TOPS-Problem Solving Program, The Mathworks* and *How to Solve Story Problems.*

WHY ENRICHMENT MATH?

Enrichment and parental involvement are both crucial parts of children's education. More school systems are recognizing that this part of the educational process is crucial to school success. Enrichment activities give children the opportunity to practice basic skills and that encourages them to think mathematically. That's exactly the kind of opportunity children get when doing *ENRICHMENT MATH.*

One of the important goals of *ENRICHMENT MATH* is to increase children's involvement in mathematics and mathematical concepts. When children are involved in mathematics activities, they become more alert and receptive to learning. They understand more. They remember more. Games, puzzles, and "hands-on" activities that lead to mathematical discoveries are guaranteed to get children involved in mathematics. That's why such activities form the core of each *ENRICHMENT MATH* lesson.

Another important goal of *ENRICHMENT MATH* is to provide opportunities for parents to become involved in their children's education. Every *ENRICHMENT MATH* lesson has two parts. First, there is a lesson that the children do on their own. Second, there is a game or an activity that the child does with an adult. *ENRICHMENT MATH* doesn't ask parents to teach children. Instead the program asks parents to play math games and engage in interesting math activities with their children.

Published in 1995 by AMERICAN EDUCATION PUBLISHING
© 1991 SRA/McGraw-Hill

HOW TO USE ENRICHMENT MATH

Each *ENRICHMENT MATH* section consists of 31 lessons on perforated sheets. On the front of each sheet, there is an activity that the child completes independently. On the back there is a follow-up activity for the child to complete with an adult. These group activities include games, projects, puzzles, surveys and trivia quizzes. The front and back pages of a lesson focus on the same mathematical skill.

Activities may be done at the time the skills are being taught to provide additional practice, or used at a later date to maintain skill levels.

Within each level, the lessons are organized into four or five sections. These sections correspond to the major mathematical topics emphasized at the particular grade level. This means you can quickly locate a lesson on whatever topic you want at whatever level is appropriate for your child.

TEACHING SUGGESTIONS
Grade 3
Optional Activities

A TIP FOR SUCCESS

Children will find *ENRICHMENT MATH* Grade 3 assignments enjoyable and easy to understand. Although each lesson has simple and easy-to-read instructions, you may wish to spend a few minutes explaining some lessons before assigning the material. You might even do some of the activities prior to giving the assignments. Many of the activities can liven up an at-home math session and will prepare your child for even greater success.

Part One: Computation–Basic Facts

ENRICHMENT MATH Grade 3 has five lessons on the basic facts. Traditionally, grade 3 is the level at which students should master the basic addition and subtraction facts and begin to address the challenge of mastering the basic multiplication and division facts.

The first two lessons in this section deal with basic addition and subtraction facts and are appropriate for use at the beginning of the school year. You may wish to introduce the first lesson, *Target Sum*, by writing a sum, any number from 0 to 18, and asking your child to give all the pairs of addends with this sum. The games provided in these lessons, or some variations of them, can be used throughout the year to help your child master and retain the basic addition and subtraction facts.

The second pair of lessons in this section deal with basic multiplication and division facts and are appropriate for use whenever your child is studying these facts. The lesson *Nines-By-Fingers* presents a mechanical way to find products when multiplying by 9. As a follow-up to this lesson, you may want your child to look for a pattern in the digits that name the product of 9 and another whole number: The sum of the digits is always nine. This discovery will help students master their multiplication facts with 9 as a factor.

The game *Roll-A-Product* can be used often throughout the year as an enjoyable way to practice the basic multiplication facts. A variation of the game that includes all of the basic facts can be created as follows. Use 20 small squares of paper to make 2 sets of playing pieces on which you have written the digits from 0 to 9. The playing pieces are placed face down and players take turns selecting two and multiplying the numbers drawn. The product should be written on a playing board if the appropriate space is empty. Different playing boards can be made by drawing a 5 x 5 array of boxes and filling in the top row and left column with any 4 digits chosen at random. Your child should use a different card for each new game so that he or she eventually practices all of the facts.

Part Two: Place Value and Operations with Whole Numbers

This section of *ENRICHMENT MATH* Grade 3 extends computational work with whole numbers from basic facts to adding and subtracting up to 4-digit numbers and multiplying and dividing 2-digit numbers by 1-digit numbers. Through a series of interesting puzzles, games, and quizzes, your child is provided with numerous opportunities to improve his or her skills with basic operations. Some of the games, such as *199* and *Divvy Up*, can be used thoughout the year as an interesting way to practice and maintain computational skills.

This part of the program also gives attention to the concept of place value, important for children to understand because of its importance to the procedures, or algorithms, utilized when computing with numbers larger than a single digit. You might choose to allow your child to play the game *Place It Right* throughout the year as free time permits. Variations of the game can be devised, if you wish. For example, your child can pick four cards and with them name the greatest and the least numbers possible. Another variation, after adding or subtracting of 2-digit numbers has been introduced and practiced, is to use the four cards to name two 2-digit addends that have the greatest sum or the least sum.

Part Three: Measurement and Geometry

Six lessons are included in this section that deal with measurement concepts such as time, metric units, and customary units and geometric concepts such as coordinate graphing, symmetry, and the identification of shapes. These lessons can be used any time.

The first three lessons are designed to help your child develop a sense of the concepts and skills involved in measurement. One of the important objectives is to help children to develop a mental model of a unit of measure. For example, in the lesson *Measure Up*, children use a piece of string one meter, or less than one meter in length. Once found, a mental picture of these objects can be kept in mind and used when needed in the future to compare with and estimate the length of other objects.

Part Four: Fractions and Decimals

The first two lessons in this section deal with fractional parts of an object and fractional parts of a set. An extension of these lessons would be to have your child separate a circle or square or other geometric figure into fractional parts and to color the parts to create an interesting design.

The lesson on *Fraction Shapes* and *A Capital Quiz* provides interesting practice with equivalent fractions, an important concept for children to understand in order to add and subtract unlike fractions at a later point in their studies.

The next two lessons present activities with decimals, including adding and subtracting decimals. The final lesson on amounts of money is included at this point since our monetary system is primarily a decimal system, and a better understanding of one system reinforces understanding of the other.

Part Five: Problem Solving

The final six lessons in *ENRICHMENT MATH* Grade 3 address problem solving. The first two lessons deal with information found in tables or graphs. This is particularly important for a child to understand since much of the information that is made available to citizens today is done through graphical devices such as tables and bar graphs. The lesson *What Color Cars Go By* introduces children to one way that data are collected and recorded.

To complete the activities in the remaining lessons, children will apply logical reasoning, use their number sense, write their own problems, and apply the problem-solving strategy of guess and check. It is important that the strategy guess-and-check be introduced at an early level so that children can begin to see the difference between "wild" guesses and "intelligent" guesses and to learn how to look for patterns in the results of their guesses in order to make their next guess a more appropriate one.

Answer Key
Grade 3–ENRICHMENT MATH

page 11:

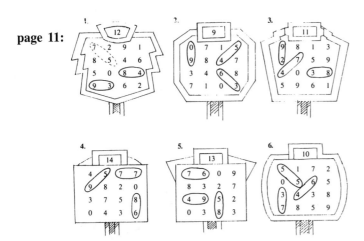

page 12: answers will vary.

page 13: 1. 8 2. 6 3. 4 4. 18 5. 13 6. 9
7. 16 8. 0 9. 11 10. 7 11. 12
12. 8, 5

page 14: answers will vary.

page 15: 1. 45 2. 6 3. 72 4. 81 5. 27 6. 54

page 16:

Playing Board

×	1	2	3	4	5	6
1	1	2	3	4	5	6
2	2	4	6	8	10	12
3	3	6	9	12	15	18
4	4	8	12	16	20	24
5	5	10	15	20	25	30
6	6	12	18	24	30	36

page 17:

1.

24	÷	6	=	4
÷		÷		÷
8	÷	2	=	4
=		=		=
3	÷	3	=	1

2.

36	÷	6	=	6
÷		÷		÷
9	÷	3	=	3
=		=		=
6	÷	2	=	3

3.

48	÷	6	=	8
÷		÷		÷
8	÷	2	=	4
=		=		=
6	÷	3	=	2

4.

40	÷	4	=	10
÷		÷		÷
8	÷	4	=	2
=		=		=
5	÷	1	=	5

page 18: 1. answers will vary 2. 4
3. answers will vary 4. 5
5. answers will vary 6. 5

page 19: 1. $7 \times 4 = 28$; $9 \times 6 = 54$
2. $9 + 7 = 16$; $18 \div 6 = 3$
3. $12 - 5 = 7$; $13 - 9 = 4$
4. $24 \div 8 = 3$; $7 + 4 = 11$
5. $8 \times 0 = 0$; $36 \div 6 = 6$

page 20: answers will vary

page 21:

1.

5	+	7	=	12
×		+		−
3	×	2	=	6
=		=		=
15	−	9	=	6

2.

18	÷	6	=	3
÷		−		+
2	×	4	=	8
=		=		=
9	+	2	=	11

3.

7	×	2	=	14
+		×		+
6	÷	3	=	2
=		=		=
13	−	6	=	7

4.

24	÷	3	=	8
÷		−		−
6	+	2	=	3
=		=		=
4	+	1	=	5

page 22: answers will vary

page 23: 1. 3782 2. 4590 3. 9852 4. 1627
5. 6534 6. 9107

page 24: with any set of 4 number cards you can make
24 different numbers.

page 25: 1. bus 2. toy car, van 3. truck, dune
buggy 4. taxi, van 5. truck, bus, dune
buggy 6. vans

page 26: answers will vary

page 27: answers will vary

page 28: 1. 112; whale shark 2. 143; ostrich
3. 616; St. Bernard 4. 1853; goby
5. 1200; Helena's hummingbird
6. 7000; yorkshire terrier

page 29:

¹1	9	²1		³4	5
3		⁴7	9	6	
2		8		⁵5	3
⁶4	⁷9				6
	⁸8	⁹7	¹⁰2		¹¹6
¹²6	0	5	3		2
	1		¹³4	2	9

page 30: answers will vary

page 31: 1. 3 2. 4 3. 8 4. 5 5. 7 6. 9

page 32: 1. $34 \times 2 = 68$ 2. $15 \times 3 = 45$
3. $14 \times 5 = 70$ 4. $26 \times 3 = 78$

page 33: 1. 44 2. 30 3. 50 4. 32 5. 36
6. 42 7. 32 8. 18 9. kangaroo
10. pig, opposum, hedge hog, dog

page 34: answers will vary

page 35:

START	ARROWS	STOP		START	ARROWS	STOP
2	↑	12		3	↑	13
14	↑	24		35	↑↑	55
38	↑	48		64	↓↓	44
15	→	16		32	→→	35
31	→	32		76	→→→	73
42	←	41		7	↑↑→	26
57	←	56		52	↓↓↓↓→→	14
25	↓	15		19	↑↑↑↑↑↑→→→	85
39	↓→	30		22	↑→→	34
6	↑↑	26		98	↓↓↓↓→→	56
21	↓→→	13		62	↑↑↑→→→→	95
80	↓↓↓←	49		16	↑↑↑↑↑	66
38	↑↑↑→	69		37	↑↑↑↑↑→→→	80

page 36: answers will vary

page 37: 1. 8 2. 30 3. 22 4. 6 5. 26 6. 21

page 38: answers will vary

page 39: answers will vary

page 40: 1. 300 2. 91 3. 160 4. 270 5. 340
6. 400 7. 61 8. 46

page 41: 1. years 2. pounds 3. feet 4. days
5. quart 6. miles 7. minutes 8. hours

page 42: answers will vary

page 43:

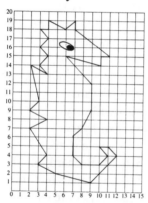

page 44: answers will vary

page 45: 1. answers will vary
2. I, O, T, U, V, W, X, Y
3. answers will vary   4. answers will
vary   5. D, H, I, O, X   6. answers
will vary

page 46: answers will vary

page 47: 1. 3¢ 2. 1¢ 3. 5¢ 4. 8¢ 5. 8¢
6. 11¢ 7. 18¢ 8. 14¢ 9. 23¢

page 48: 1. RED 2. CAT 3. ROSE 4. DIME
5. JOHN 6. PEAR

page 49: THEY BOTH ARE RULERS; THEY BOTH
HAVE PENS.

page 50: answers will vary

page 51: 1. circles 2. squares 3. circles
4. triangles 5. triangles 6. squares

page 52: 2. HEat 3. You 4. BOard 5. THat
6. HAd 7. VESt 8. CALling
9. datES;... THEY BOTH HAVE SCALES.

page 53:

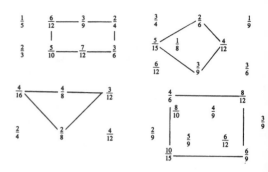

page 54: 1. $\frac{4}{6}$ Helena   2. $\frac{6}{12}$ Atlanta
3. $\frac{3}{15}$ Boston   4. $\frac{9}{12}$ Columbus
5. $\frac{4}{10}$ Juneau   6. $\frac{2}{12}$ Austin
7. $\frac{3}{9}$ Columbia   8. $\frac{2}{16}$ Denver
9. $\frac{2}{8}$ Sacramento   10. $\frac{10}{12}$ Dover

page 55: 1. 5.7 2. 6.9 3. 14.2 4. 25.1
5. 8.17 6. 9.36 7. 15.04 8. 47.82
9. 8.7 10. 60.43 11. 70.05
12. 14.02 13. 5.07 14. 10.1
15. 20.10; Mystery number is 20.01.

page 56: 1. There are 5 rings.   2. There are 4
pins.   3. The distance is 90 feet.
4. The field is 120 yards long.   5. Hank
Aaron

page 57: 1. 4.2; 3.1 2. 5.9; 1.1 3. 0.7; 1.8
4. 9.1; 2.9 5. 5.08; 1.24
6. 2.99; 2.92

page 58: answers will vary

page 59: 1. 22¢ 2. 41¢ 3. 76¢ 4. 45¢
5. 46¢ 6. 38¢

page 60: answers will vary

page 61: 1. 714 2. 548 3. Frank Robinson
4. Hank Aaron 5. 87 6. 166

page 62: answers will vary

page 63: 1. 140; 90; 100 2. 160; 60 3. 110; 30
4. 190; 70

page 64: answers will vary

page 65: 1. 6847 2. 3346 3. 9822 4. 2946
5. 2136 6. 4346

page 66: answers will vary

67: 1. 11; 7; 4   2. 90; 110; 200   3. 60; 50;
   58   4. 20; 40; 38

68: 1. 2; 12; 24   2. 4; 8; 64   3. 1933; 4; 40
   4. 1500; 400; 350

69: answers will vary

70: answers will vary

71:

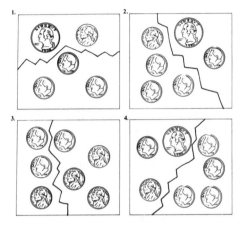

page 72:

Also available from American Education Publishing—

MASTER SKILLS SERIES SKILL BOOKS

The Master Skills Series is not just another workbook series. These full-color workbooks were designed by experts who understand the value of reinforcing basic skills! Subjects include Reading, Math, English, Comprehension, Spelling and Writing, and Thinking Skills.

• **88 pages**   • **40 titles**   • **All-color**   • **$5.95 each**

TEACHING SUGGESTIONS
Grade 4
Optional Activities

A TIP FOR SUCCESS

Children will find *ENRICHMENT MATH* Grade 4 lessons enjoyable and easy to understand. Although each lesson has simple and easy-to-read instructions, you may wish to spend a few minutes explaining some lessons before assigning the material. You might even do some of the activities prior to giving the assignments. Many of the activities can liven up an at-home math session and will prepare your child for even greater success.

Part One: Place Value and Operations with Basic Facts

ENRICHMENT MATH Grade 4 begins with six lessons on basic facts. The first lesson offers activities on basic addition and subtraction facts. Although children are expected to have mastered these facts by the end of grade 3, there usually are some who have not yet done so. Plus, children can always benefit from further practice designed to increase their speed of recall. You might note that the game *Middle of the Path* can be used often throughout the year to help your child become more proficient with basic addition and subtraction facts.

The second lesson offers activities on basic multiplication and division facts. These facts were introduced and practiced in grade 3, and children should strive to master the facts by the end of grade 4. Such mastery is critical, for example, for success with the difficult skill of long division, introduced at this grade level. One way to extend the practice provided in *ENRICHMENT MATH* Grade 3 is to suggest that, after children do *Who's Who*, they find similar facts in social studies or science and write their own riddles in code for other children to solve.

The next two lessons provide practice activities using all four basic operations, and the last two lessons deal with place value and rounding. The concept of place value is important to understand since it is involved in virtually all of the procedures, or algorithms, used to add, subtract, multiply, and divide numbers greater than those named by a single digit. The game *Digit Derby* can be used again and again any time throughout the year when you determine that more practice with the concept would be beneficial. The concept of rounding is useful when estimating, an important skill, and the game *Roll and Round*, which involves the concept of place value as well as that of rounding, also can be used again and again any time throughout the year. You may wish to vary the game by changing the rules on the game cards to round to the nearest hundred, to the nearest ten thousand, and so forth.

Part Two: Operations with Whole Numbers

The seven lessons in this section of *ENRICHMENT MATH* Grade 4 extend operations with whole numbers from basic facts to adding and subtracting up to 4-digit numbers and multiplying and dividing up to 3-digit numbers.

Some children simply need more time or more practice to become proficient in the skills addressing this section, and these children will be particular beneficiaries as a result of doing the activities. You should note also that many of the activities included in this section can be extended by having children make their own activity sheets similar to the original. For example, more activities similar to those in *The Product is the Fruit* can be developed by asking your child to select the name of a fruit and then create the multiplication exercises that other children will solve to crack the code. As another variation of this game, you should note that the exercises could be addition or subtraction as well as multiplication.

The first lesson in the division sequence, *Estimating Quotients*, addresses an important part of the long division process. You might want to introduce the lesson by identifying for your child what a decade is, showing the different division exercises similar to those on the activity sheet, and then asking your child to tell what decade the quotient is in. For example, the quotient for 690 ÷ 30 in between 20 and 30.

Part Three: Measurement and Geometry

This section dealing with measurement and geometry begins with a lesson on elapsed time. By doing the activities in this lesson, children will gain a sense of different periods of time, thereby improving their ability to estimate how long an event may take to occur.

The next two lessons deal with metric units and customary units respectively. One important objective of these lessons is to help children develop and retain a mental image of some object that they can use at any time as a standard for estimating the measure of some other object. For example, if they remember that a sheet of paper is about 1 foot long, they can mentally compare the unknown width of a room with the number of sheets of paper that would be needed to equal this length and come up with a reasonable estimate.

The remaining lessons provide interesting opportunities to gain a better understanding of the concepts of perimeter, area, and volume. Such activities are valuable experiences for those children who often simply memorize formulas without having any understanding of the important underlying concepts.

Part Four: Fractions and Decimals

The first two lessons in this section deal with finding or identifying equivalent fractions and mixed numbers. The ability to do this properly is a required subskill for success in adding and subtracting fractions or mixed numbers that do not have a common denominator. You may choose to introduce the first activity, *Geography Quiz*, by writing four fractions, only three of which are equivalent and asking your child to identify the fraction that does not belong. This activity can be repeated throughout the year.

The lesson *Decimal Number Logic* begins a series of activities dealing with place value in decimals. A sound understanding of this concept will do much to insure success when doing more advanced work with decimals. Children should recognize that the place-value pattern in decimals is the same as it is in whole numbers, and that the decimal point is not a place but simply identifies the ones place in the number. The game *Decimal Tournament* can be used throughout the year to reinforce the understanding of place value.

Part Five: Problem Solving

The first lesson in this section not only helps children to interpret information provided on a road sign or a map, the activities also serve to sharpen each child's ability to analyze the situation and the available data in order to solve a problem.

The problem solving strategy of guess and check, utilized in the second lesson of this section, is probably used more often in real life than most people realize. Therefore, activities such as those presented here will help children learn how to make intelligent guesses and to look for a pattern in the results to help them make their next more-informed guess.

The activities in the next two lessons require a child to analyze the situation and apply his or her number sense to solve a probem. The development of such abilities in a young person is not a simple task or something that can be achieved in a short period of time. But by utilizing these lessons, you should feel confident that you have made a valuable contribution to the achievement of an important goal.

page 75: 1. 9¢ 2. 11¢ 3. 17¢ 4. 13¢ 5. 7¢
6. 4¢ 7. 8¢ 8. 1¢

page 76: answers will vary

page 77: 1. Louis Braille 2. John Glenn

page 78: 1. 3 2. 24 3. 2 4. 6 5. 5 6. 5
7. 1 8. 8

page 79: 1. 8;7 2. 9;3 3. 3;12 4. 6;4
5. 6;6 6. 3;8 7. 7;6 8. 5;7
9. 8;8

page 80: answers will vary

page 81: 1. 1 2. 18 3. 12 4. 3 5. 36
6. 13 7. 0 8. 7 9. 9 10. 2
11. 8 12. 17 13. 27 14. 14
15. 5 16. 6

page 82: answers will vary. Possible answers given.
1. $2+2+2-3-3=0$
2. $2+2-3=1$
3. $3+3-2-2=2$
4. $3+2-2=3$
5. $2+2+3-3=4$
6. $2+3=5$
7. $2\div2+3+2=6$
8. $3\times2+3-2=7$
9. $3+3+3+2-3=8$
10. $3\times2+3=9$

page 83:

¹3	²2	6	³3	4	5	.
	3		0		⁴8	
⁵5	0	3	2	⁶6	9	
	0		⁷4	3	⁸3	⁹3
¹⁰9	0	4		2		8
¹¹2	1		¹²7	1	0	3	2
7				8		5
¹³3	9	5		¹⁴4	8	5	6

page 84: answers will vary

page 85: 1. 3889 2. 5163 3. 9499 4. 1527
5. 13,497 6. 56,001 7. 60,862
8. 89,500 9. 7358 or 7385
10. 6812 or 6821

page 86: answers will vary

page 87: 1. C 2. B 3. D 4. A 5. C 6. B
7. A 8. C 9. D 10. B 11. A
12. B 13. C 14. B 15. D

page 88: answers will vary

page 89:

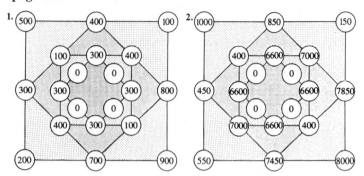

page 90: answers will vary

page 91: 1. 5 2. 32 3. 74 4. 8 5. 65 6. 2
7. 647 8. 7

page 92: answers will vary

page 93: 1. pineapple 2. cantaloupe

page 94: answers will vary

page 95: 1. 10 2. 31 3. 12 4. 26 5. 132
6. 100 7. 102 8. 50 9. 40 10. 88

page 96: 1. 21; The flag had 13 stars.
2. 18; There are 100 senators.
3. 14; There are 9 justices.
4. 413; Hancock was 39 years old.
5. 214; Washington, D.C. was chosen
in 1790.

page 97: 1. 40 2. 20 3. 70 4. 10 5. 30
6. 20

page 98: 1. George Washington
2. Thomas Jefferson
3. Andrew Jackson
4. Abraham Lincoln
5. Franklin Roosevelt
6. Dwight Eisenhower
7. John Kennedy
8. Ronald Reagan

page 99: 1. 300 2. 300 3. 350 4. 300
5. 441 6. 441 7. 1441 8. 441
9. 325 10. 324 11. 325 12. 325
13. 506 14. 496 15. 496 16. 496

page 100: answers will vary

page 101: 1. 3:45; Carol jogged to the park.
2. 5:00; John practiced the piano.
3. 4:40; Bob played basketball.
4. 5:10; Sue saw a movie.
5. 11:55; Ken baked bread.
6. 2:53; Ann biked to the store.

page 102: answers will vary

page 103: 1. EAR 2. TOSS 3. REST
4. POLE 5. REAL 6. PLATE
7. TASTE 8. STREET

page 104: answers will vary

page 105:

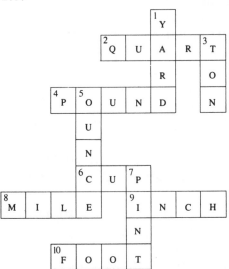

page 106: answers will vary

page 107: 1. triangle 2. square 3. hexagon
4. octagon 5. quadrilateral
6. pentagon

page 108: answers will vary. Possible answers given.

1. Remove 2 toothpicks. Leave 3 squares.

2. Remove 4 toothpicks. Leave 2 squares.

3. Remove 4 toothpicks. Leave 4 squares.

4. Remove 5 toothpicks. Leave 4 squares.

5. Remove 8 toothpicks. Leave 5 squares.

6. Remove 4 toothpicks. Leave 5 squares.

page 109: 1. 28 2. 12 3. 15 4. 16
5. refreshments 6. Seal Pool
7. Children's Park
8. Children's Park and the Bird House

page 110: answers will vary. Possible answers are given:

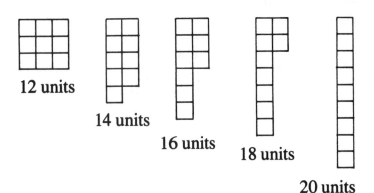

12 units

14 units

16 units

18 units

20 units

page 111: 1. $11 2. $24 3. $20 4. $30
5. $10 6. $30

page 112: THEY BOTH ARE GROUND.

page 113: 1. $\frac{3}{8}$ Kansas 2. $\frac{3}{20}$ Ohio
3. $\frac{4}{5}$ Colorado 4. $\frac{2}{11}$ Nebraska
5. $\frac{24}{42}$ Mississippi 6. $\frac{1}{4}$ Iowa

page 114: 1. $\frac{4}{7}$ 2. $\frac{3}{6}$ 3. $\frac{4}{10}$ 4. $\frac{4}{15}$ 5. $\frac{4}{9}$
6. $\frac{6}{12}$ 7. $\frac{3}{8}$ 8. $\frac{6}{8}$—SUPERMAN

page 115: 1. $2\frac{1}{2}$ 2. $2\frac{1}{3}$ 3. $2\frac{3}{4}$ 4. $1\frac{3}{10}$
5. 2 6. $2\frac{1}{6}$ 7. $1\frac{2}{5}$ 8. $5\frac{1}{3}$
9. 6 10. 4 11. 3 12. $1\frac{1}{8}$
13. $1\frac{1}{10}$ 14. $2\frac{5}{6}$ 15. $1\frac{5}{8}$

THERE ARE 5 PIPES ON A BAGPIPE.

page 116: 1. $2\frac{2}{3}$ Land of the Midnight Sun
2. $1\frac{1}{2}$ Grand Canyon State
3. $2\frac{1}{4}$ Golden State
4. $1\frac{1}{6}$ Sunshine State
5. 4 Peach State
6. $3\frac{3}{5}$ Bluegrass State
7. $3\frac{1}{3}$ Magnolia State
8. 5 Treasure State
9. $1\frac{5}{6}$ Garden State
10. $8\frac{1}{2}$ Beehive State

page 117: THOMAS EDISON
page 118: 1; $\frac{1}{4}$, $\frac{3}{4}$, $\frac{1}{2}$, 1; 2; $\frac{1}{4}$, 2

page 119: 1. 246.3   2. 501.2   3. 58.39
          4. 74.78   5. 765.09   6. 627.48
page 120: answers will vary
page 121:

Race Results	
Name	Time (in seconds)
Kim	13.05
Julio	12.45
Maria	12.56
Tony	13.0
Richard	14.3
Lisa	14.25

page 122: answers will vary
page 123: 1. 3   2. 1   3. 5   4. 9
page 124: answers will vary
page 125: 1. 53   2. 135   3. 23   4. 75   5. 58
          6. 2   7. 68   8. 40

page 126:

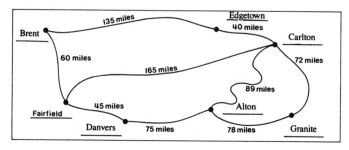

page 127: 1. socks–$2.50
          2. Sweatshirt–$12.50; T-shirt–$5.50
          3. Sweatpants–$9.00; T-shirt–$5.50
          4. Jogging shoes–$22.00;
          sweatshirt–$12.50;
          Sweatpants–$9.00   5. Jogging shoes–
          $22.00; T-shirt–$5.50; Socks–$2.50
          6. Socks–$2.50; Sweatpants–$9.00;
          Jogging shoes–$22.00

page 128: Column I: 1 penny; 5; 3 runs; 0   Column II:
          4 nickels, 9 years old; 33; 12
page 129: 1. 30   2. 52   3. 15   4. 244   5. 330
page 130: answers will vary
page 131: 1. 300; 50; 10   2. $8.50; $2.50; $3.25;
          $22.75   3. $5; $3; $1; $20   4. $1.80;
          $3.60; $0.90; $2.75

page 132: 1. 30; 110; 150   2. 183; 61; 180; 42
page 133: answers will vary
page 134: answers will vary.
page 135: 1. 236 people   2. 102 moon rocks
          3. 2:00   4. $2.55
page 136: answers will vary

Enrichment
READING

Grades 3 & 4
Answer Key and Teaching Suggestions

AMERICAN EDUCATION PUBLISHING

READING OVERVIEW

ENRICHMENT READING is designed to provide children with practice in reading and to increase their reading abilities. The major areas of reading instruction—word skills, vocabulary, study skills, comprehension, and literary forms—are covered as appropriate at each level.

ENRICHMENT READING provides a wide range of activities that target a variety of skills in each instructional area. The program is unique because it helps children expand their skills in playful ways with games, puzzles, riddles, contests, and stories. The high-interest activities are informative and fun to do.

Home involvement is important to any child's success in school. *ENRICHMENT READING* is the ideal vehicle for fostering home involvement. Every lesson provides specific opportunities for children to work with a parent, a family member, an adult, or a friend.

AUTHORS

Peggy Kaye, the author of *ENRICHMENT READING*, is also an author of *ENRICHMENT MATH* and the author of two parent/teacher resource books, *Games for Reading* and *Games for Math.* Currently, Ms. Kaye divides her time between writing books and tutoring students in reading and math. She has also taught for ten years in New York City public and private schools.

WRITERS

Timothy J. Baehr is a writer and editor of instructional materials on the elementary, secondary, and college levels. Mr. Baehr has also authored an award-winning column on bicycling and a resource book for writers of educational materials.

Cynthia Benjamin is a writer of reading instructional materials, television scripts, and original stories. Ms. Benjamin has also tutored students in reading at the New York University Reading Institute.

Russell Ginns is a writer and editor of materials for a children's science and nature magazine. Mr. Ginn's speciality is interactive materials, including games, puzzles, and quizzes.

WHY ENRICHMENT READING?

Enrichment and parental involvement are both crucial to children's success in school, and educators recognize the important role work done at home plays in the educational process. Enrichment activities give children opportunities to practice, apply, and expand their reading skills, while encouraging them to think while they read. *ENRICHMENT READING* offers exactly this kind of opportunity. Each lesson focuses on an important reading skill and involves children in active learning. Each lesson will entertain and delight children.

When children enjoy their lessons and are involved in the activities, they are naturally alert and receptive to learning. They understand more. They remember more. All children enjoy playing games, having contests, and solving puzzles. They like reading interesting stories, amusing stories, jokes, and riddles. Activities such as these get children involved in reading. This is why these kinds of activities form the core of *ENRICHMENT READING*.

Each lesson consists of two parts. Children complete the first part by themselves. The second part is completed together with a family member, an adult, or a friend.

ENRICHMENT READING activities do not require people at home to teach reading. Instead, the activities involve everyone in enjoyable reading games and interesting language experiences.

Published in 1995 by AMERICAN EDUCATION PUBLISHING
© 1991 SRA/McGraw-Hill

HOW TO USE HOMEWORK READING

Each *ENRICHMENT READING* section consists of 31 two-page lessons. Each page of a lesson is one assignment. Children complete the first page independently. They complete the second page with a family member, an adult, or a friend. The two pages of a lesson focus on the same reading skill or related skills.

Each level is organized into four or five units emphasizing the major areas of reading instruction appropriate to the level of the book. This means you will always have the right lesson available for the curriculum requirements of your child.

The *ENRICHMENT READING* lessons may be completed in any order. They may be used to provide practice at the same time skills are introduced at school, or they may be used to review skills at a later date.

The games and activities in *ENRICHMENT READING* are useful additions to any classroom or home reading program. In many cases, your child's answers will vary according to his or her own thoughts, perceptions, and experiences. Always accept any reasonable answers your child gives.

TEACHING SUGGESTIONS
Grade 3
Optional Activities

A TIP FOR SUCCESS

Children using Grade 3 of *ENRICHMENT READING* will find the games and activities easy to understand and fun to complete. It is a good idea, however, to take a few minutes to explain the assignments. You might also try doing some of the activities and playing some of the games. When children are familiar with the directions and know what is expected of them, they are more likely to complete their work successfully, and the games and activities will add some playful learning to children's reading experiences.

Word Skills

The Word Skills unit contains seven lessons which cover basic decoding skills. Included are lessons on consonants, vowels, syllabication, word endings, compound words, and contractions.

The first three lessons deal with consonant and vowel sounds. You may use the first lesson to provide your child with practice in both short and long vowels. The second lesson concentrates on vowel diphthongs and digraphs, while the third lesson focuses on consonant blends and digraphs. The second page of each lesson is a game. The games will enable you to assign enjoyable word skills practice all year long.

By the time children are using Grade 3, their reading materials often require them to read long words. Children who are able to break words into syllables usually have an easier time sounding out longer words. The activities in Lesson 4 provide children with playful ways to practice their syllabication skills.

Many young children have difficulty with the various plural endings and inflectional endings for words. Two imaginative activities, a drawing activity and an activity with information about bees, and two games will help you provide your child with practice in using these word skills. If your child enjoys playing *Color Three* (page 148) and *Word Collector* (page 150), you may wish to create new game boards with new words for your child to use at home. You might also encourage your child to make his or her own game boards. Help your child research the words and make the game boards.

Study Skills

The Study Skills unit contains two lessons covering dictionary skills. Although children Grade Level 3 will have had some experience using a dictionary, this is also the time when more direct instruction in how to use a dictionary begins.

A full understanding of alphabetical order is crucial to developing good dictionary skills, but many children are bored by exercises that merely ask them to alphabetize words. Lesson 8 takes the boredom away. Most children love to do dot-to-dot drawings, and when words replace the numbers, children enjoy the activity just as much. After your child completes *Follow the Alphabet* (page 153), you may want to adapt some ready-made dot-to-dot drawings by substituting alphabetized words for the numbers.

Children will especially enjoy *Alphabet Code* (page 154) because codes intrigue them. You can make up any number of variations on this activity. Try having children engage in a code speed contest. Call out a word and have children race to put the word into alphabetical order code. The first child to finish says, "Code cracker." Then he or she writes the coded word on the chalkboard. If everyone agrees the word has been properly coded, the child gets one point.

Another important dictionary skill involves becoming familiar with dictionary entries. *Dictionary Mystery* (page 155) and *Dictionary Numbers* (page 156) provide practice with this skill. Here is a variation on *Dictionary Numbers* to use with groups of four children. Give each child four blank cards on which to write dictionary entries. Have each child write an entry word on one card, the pronunciation on another card, a definition on another card, and a sample sentence on the last card. Encourage children to look in the dictionary when making their cards, and provide help as needed. When the children are finished, collect all the cards and shuffle them together. Then deal four cards to each player. Say "Go," and have each player pass one card to the player on the right. Now everyone has a new hand of cards. Let the players inspect their cards, and if one player has a complete dictionary entry, she or he wins the game. If no one has a complete entry, say "Go" again, and have the players pass along another card. Children should continue playing until one player comes up with a complete entry and wins the game.

Vocabulary

The Vocabulary unit contains seven lessons designed to help children develop their vocabularies and increase their general word knowledge. The first lesson focuses on antonyms and synonyms. After completing *An Opposites Poem* (page 157), children may enjoy having an "opposites half hour" at home. During the opposite half hour, whoever speaks should try to say the opposite of what he or she really means. For example, you might say, "Do not get out your notebooks." This translates into "Get out your notebooks." Here is a harder opposite: "Thank you, no one stand up later." This translates into "Please, everyone sit down now." It may be tough living in an opposites world, but it can also be fun.

The second vocabulary lesson deals with homophones. After children complete *Riddle Time* (page 160), you may want to start a homophone riddle collection. Homophone riddles also make good material for handwriting practice. Handwriting lessons are more fun when a funny joke comes into play.

In Lesson 12, children practice using multiple meaning words. You may extend this lesson with the following game. Divide children into teams. Then think of a word with multiple meanings, such as *trip*. Do not tell the children the word. Instead, give two definitions, such as "to stumble" and "a journey," and have the teams try to guess the word. The first team to figure out the word scores one point. If everyone is stumped, give a context sentence using the definitions, such as, "I took a journey to the North Pole and stumbled upon a polar bear." Then let the teams try again to guess the word.

When skillful readers come across unknown words, they can often figure out the meaning of the words from how they are used in the text. To do this, children need to become adept at using context clues. *The Wrong Words* (page 163) and *What's Next?* (page 164) provide children with playful practice in using context clues. To extend these activities, you might try this game. Select a short piece of writing with good context clues. Make a copy and cross out or blank out words in the story that can be figured out from the context. Then make copies for the children and challenge them to replace the words. Each student gets one point for every word she or he replaces correctly. The child or children with the most points wins.

This Leads to That (page 167) and *Shared Thinking* (page 168) give children opportunities to make simple semantic maps. After children complete the activities, encourage them to share their word lists. You may all be surprised by how many different words are included.

Comprehension

The Comprehension unit contains eleven lessons covering all the aspects of comprehension appropriate to Grade 3. The main goal of the games and activities is to help children become actively engaged in reading. You can help by talking about the lessons with your child. When children have opportunities to talk about their work, they feel that their thoughts are important.

To begin, children get practice in finding main ideas and supporting details and in following directions. If your child particularly enjoys *Do As I Say* (page 174), he or she may also enjoy making up his or her own sets of directions and playing the game with others.

Some of the games and activities focus on evaluation and higher order thinking skills, and several of them encourage children to use their imaginations to come up with original responses to open-ended questions. After children complete *Whose Restaurant?* (page 175), encourage them to share their answers. Children may then enjoy making one or more of the dishes listed on the menus, including the specials they added. For the Monster Cafe, children can make the foods out of craft materials. For the two other restaurants, simple recipes can be found and prepared by one child or a group of children. Children may also enjoy playing *Spin a Tale* (page 192). Encourage children to add their own problems, characters, and settings to the lists in order to increase the story possibilities. Make sure children also make additional number cards for the items added to the lists.

Several lessons contain scientific or historical information. If children express particular interest in pyramids, ecology, black holes, giraffes, or elephants, be sure to encourage them to explore these subjects further. There are many appropriate level books on these subjects in libraries and bookstores.

Forms of Writing

The Forms of Writing unit contains four lessons that help children develop appreciation for several different forms of written material. The areas covered are history, mathematics, newspapers, poetry, fairy tales, and tall tales.

After completing *Number Tricks* (page 194), your child may want to do the tricks several times to make sure they work every time.

Before you assign *Poem Day* (page 197), make sure your child understands that not all poems rhyme. In *A Pocket's Poem* (page 198), children have the opportunity to read a delightful poem. They may also enjoy memorizing the poem and reciting it or acting it out in class.

After children complete *That's Impossible* (page 200), they may enjoy drawing pictures to illustrate their favorite boasts. They will also most likely want to have more boasting contests with their friends and family members. This interest can be taken advantage of by exposing children to a variety of tall tales and having them identify the exaggerated and unbelievable elements.

Answer Key
Grade 3–Enrichment Reading

Page 139 1. kite 2. boat 3. pen 4. leaf 5. cane 6. pot 7. rip 8. nail 9. tie 10. hat 11. rose 12. beet; A cricket hears with its legs.

Page 140 Results will vary.

Page 141 *Possible words:* bow, cow, how, low, mow, now, row, tow, vow, clown, down, frown, gown, town; boy, joy, toy, loyal, royal; coin, join, boil, coil, foil, soil; blouse, house, mouse, aloud, cloud, loud, proud

Page 142 Words will vary.

Page 143 *Circled words:* crisp, crust, dream, drip, free, lamp, paint, silk, sweet, swing

Page 144 Words will vary.

Page 145 Names will vary.

Page 146 Results will vary.

Page 147 1. chairs 2. peaches 3. leaves 4. berries 5. bodies; answers will vary

Page 148 *Top row:* shelves, daisies, slices *Middle row:* elbows, ashes, children *Bottom row:* bakeries, tasks, speeches

Page 149 *Lines connect:* shine–shines–shining, gleam–gleams–gleaming, glow–glows–glowing, fly–flies–flying, blaze–blazed–blazing

Page 150 Results will vary.

Page 151 Words and pictures will vary.

Page 152 *Lines between:* we've–we have, it'll–it will, who's–who is, doesn't–does not, you've–you have, wouldn't–would not, you're–you are, you'd–you would, won't–will not

Page 153 a fish

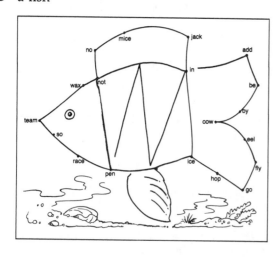

Page 154 Words will vary.

Page 155 *Entry words:* rose, rabbit, fox, piano, lake, baseball

Page 156 Results will vary.

Page 157 *Changed words:* beautiful–ugly, everyone–no one or nobody, sweet–sour, boys–girls, walk–run, backwards–forwards, whisper–shout or yell, girls–boys, big–little or small, long–short, never–always, remember–forget, won't–will, come–leave or go, here–there, out–in; answers will vary

Page 158 Results will vary.

Page 159 here, blew, see, tail, won, new, weigh, waist; 20 + 25 + 25 + 15 + 30 + 25 + 20 + 15 = 175; 175

Page 160 Answers will vary.

Page 161

Page 162 Answers will vary.

Page 163 Your heart beats one hundred thousand times every day!

Page 164 Results will vary.

Page 165 Names will vary.

Page 166 Stories and pictures will vary.

Page 167 Words and sentences will vary.

Page 168 Words and results will vary.

Page 169 *Lines between:* Red is to stop–as green is to go. Car is to road–as train is to track. Hit is to baseball–as kick is to football. Read is to book–as listen is to radio. Apple is to tree–as eggs are to hens.; cat

Page 170 paper, foot, winter, rink, bowl, hot, milk, electricity, lane, button; results will vary

Page 171 Kana; There are many kinds of lava rocks.

Page 172 *My Main Idea:* 2, 3, 6, 8 *My Friend's Main Idea:* 1, 4, 5, 7

Page 173 KEEP UP THE GOOD WORK

Page 174 Results and names will vary.

Page 175 *Left menu:* Baby Bits *Right menu:* Monster Cafe *Bottom menu:* Fitness Food *Today's specials:* answers will vary

Page 176 Answers and results will vary.

Page 177 Answers will vary, but should mention something about the pliers.

Page 178 Answers will vary.

Page 179 1. 7:50 2. red 3. Bugs and Stan 4. eating dinner 5. Stan was at a birthday party 6. Lou 7. robbing Mrs. Glow 8. Lou

Page 180 Plan 2 is in correct order; 2

Page 181 Answers will vary.

Page 182 All the statements are true.

Page 183 Answers will vary.

Page 184 Ideas will vary, but should indicate possible causes of the events.

Page 185 Answers will vary, but should tell two positive things that would be different in the story.

Page 186 Answers will vary.

Page 187 *Things wrong in picture:* dotted pants, striped shirt, five children, three-story house, wand, suitcase

Page 188 Pictures will vary, but should match the description in the story.

Page 189 Answers will vary.

Page 190 Answers will vary.

Page 191 *Plan 1:* Answers will vary, but should tell how Rosa will help Grandmother. *Plan 2:* Answers will vary, but should tell how Carlos will help the wizard get back the wand.

Page 192 Stories and pictures will vary.

Page 193 Answers will vary.

Page 194 *Trick 1:* numbers will vary *Trick 2:* 7

Page 195 Stories will vary, but answers should be appropriate to the context of the story.

Page 196 Answers will vary.

Page 197 Poems will vary.

Page 198 Ideas will vary.

Page 199 Stories will vary, but should tell how to trick an ogre.

Page 200 Boasts will vary.

TEACHING SUGGESTIONS
Grade 4
Optional Activities

A TIP FOR SUCCESS

Children are sure to enjoy using Grade 4 of *ENRICHMENT READING* because it is filled with imaginative activities, games, and puzzles. Although the directions for each lesson are easy to read and understand, you may want to spend a few minutes reviewing them. Feel free to play the games and do the activities before assigning them. The games and activities will prepare children for success with their homework as well as provide them with reading experiences that appeal to their imaginations.

Vocabulary

The Vocabulary unit contains ten lessons designed to help children expand their vocabularies and build their general word knowledge. The first lesson focuses on synonyms and antonyms. After your child plays *Wonder Wheel* (page 204), you may wish to adapt the game for family use. Make a sturdy wheel out of cardboard, and have your child contribute words for the word cards. The number and selection of word cards can be varied each time the game is played.

Lessons 2 and 3 deal with prefixes and suffixes. To give children more practice using words with affixes, try this variation of a *Round Robin* story. Begin a story with a sentence that includes at least one word with a prefix and one word with a suffix. For example, "The submarine surfaced in the middle of an amusement park filled with extraterrestrial visitors." Have children take turns adding sentences to the story. Each sentence must include at least one word with a prefix and one word with a suffix. As an added challenge, ask children to include two or more prefixes and suffixes in each sentence.

People of all ages love riddles. After your child completes *Riddles* (page 211), you may want to start a home collection of riddles. Encourage children to contribute riddles in which the answers are dependent on the context of the questions. *Color Your Sentences* (page 213) also lends itself to some enjoyable family sharing. Have your child read his or her similes and metaphors aloud. Everyone will be surprised and delighted with the variety of answers. To encourage some imaginative artwork, have your child illustrate one or more of the comparisons on the page.

After children complete *Crosswords* (page 215) and *Ladder Climb* (page 216), they may want to try their hands at making up their own analogies. If your child need more practice in categorizing after completing *Wagon Wheels* (page 217), you may wish to have him or her complete additional category wheels. Some suggested categories for the wheel centers are weather, vehicles, book characters, writing instruments, fruits, and flowers.

Monster Poem (page 219) and *One Word Leads to Another* (page 220) give children opportunities to make simple semantic maps. After your child completes page 220, encourage him or her to share his or her answers with the family. You may all be surprised by how many different words the two pictures evoked.

Study Skills

The Study Skills unit contains three lessons covering dictionary skills, maps, and graphs. A thorough understanding of alphabetical order is crucial to developing good dictionary skills, but many children are bored by exercises that merely ask them to alphabetize words. *Sentence Scramble* (page 223) takes the boredom away. Children will have fun figuring out the scrambled sentences, and since the sentences turn out to be tongue twisters, they will delight in reading the sentences aloud. Children may also wish to make up their own alphabetic scrambled sentences for family members to figure out.

Another important dictionary skill involves becoming familiar with dictionary entries. *Entry Mix-Ups* (page 225) and *Dictionary Disks* (page 226) provide practice with this skill. After children play *Dictionary Disks*, they can make their own game boards for different topics. Have children make lists of words relating to their topics, look up the words in a dictionary, and then fill in the boxes of their game boards with parts of the entries. When they play their games, children will be increasing their vocabularies as well as practicing their dictionary skills.

In *Haunted House* (page 227), children are required to use a map. To prepare for this activity, make sure your child is familiar with locating objects and places on a simple map. Also make sure your child is familiar with a map compass and where north, south, east, and west are located on a map. After your child completes page 227, he or she may enjoy making his or her own maps of real or imaginary places.

Before you assign *Word Count* (page 228), you may want to review with your child how to count items using tally marks and how to complete a simple bar graph. If your child finds this activity interesting, he or she may want to repeat it for the words *as, for, I, is, it, that* and/or for the individual letters of the alphabet.

Comprehension

The Comprehension unit contains twelve lessons covering the major aspects of comprehension appropriate to Grade 4. The first three lessons focus on finding main ideas and details. *Cross Out* (page 229) presents biographical paragraphs about four interesting youngsters. Children who express a particular interest in one or more of these youngsters might be encouraged to find out about their lives as adults. After children complete *All About Me* (page 232), they may enjoy comparing their results. Charts or graphs could also be made to record children's numbers and shapes. To extend *Time Trip* (page 233), challenge your child to describe other familiar objects in passages similar to that on page 233.

Children who recognize the play on words in the authors' names in *Where Does It Go?* (page 237) may enjoy making up additional book titles and authors to add to each bookcase. When your child works on *Consider the Facts* (page 239), encourage him to consider all the answer choices as he searches for reasons to disqualify them. *Guess Where* (page 240) and *What Happened?* (page 242) can easily be extended for home use by creating additional place descriptions and cause-and-effect sentences.

Several lessons require children to use their imaginations, rely on their own experiences and knowledge, and draw upon their previous reading experiences. Children are also asked to come up with original responses to open-ended questions. If children particularly enjoy *Mind Reader* (page 246), additional items may be added to the Item Box and a tournament or exhibition held at home.

In *Follow the Plan* (page 249), children are asked to complete a story plan and then write a story based on it. Be sure your child understands what kind of information should be included in each part of the plan, and provide help as needed if your child has difficulty organizing his or her ideas. Before *Story Map* (page 250), is assigned, you may want to introduce the activity at home and make sure children are familiar with how to complete the story map. The basic story map on page 250 may also be used whenever children read and analyze stories.

Forms of Writing

The Forms of Writing unit contains six lessons that help children develop appreciation for several different forms of written material including science, history, biography, fiction, and poetry.

Most children probably are not aware of persuasive writing techniques. To introduce Lesson 26, you may want to use some newspaper and magazine ads to help your child identify some of the persuasive techniques used. Once children become aware of this kind of writing, they will most likely find it everywhere.

After children complete *My Time Line* (page 258), they may find it interesting to compare their time lines and share their autobiographies. The activity may also spark an interest in time lines as a way of recording information. If children are interested, encourage them to make a variety of time lines, such as for their daily activities, school events, sports events, historical events, scientific events, and so on.

Shape Poems (page 261) encourages children to explore visual invention through the creation of poems shaped like what the poem tells about. In Lesson 31, children are introduced to some well-known Greek mythological figures. After children complete the lesson, you may wish to introduce them to some other myths. Children may also enjoy acting out a myth or reciting a myth in choral reading fashion.

Answer Key
Grade 4–Enrichment Reading

Page 203 Answers will vary.

Page 204 Words and results will vary.

Page 205

Page 206 Results will vary.

Page 207 beauti*fy*, pain*ter*, magic*ian*, work*able*, neighbor*hood*, mess*y*; answers will vary

Page 208 *Player 1:* discov*ery*, fear*less*, general*ly*, disappear*ance* *Player 2:* disagree*ment*, long*est*, study*ing*, creat*ed*

Page 209 1. bare 2. would 3. pane 4. weighs 5. write 6. one 7. for 8. find; blastoff

Page 210 *Top row:* pale, brakes, cent *Second row:* reign, steal, main *Third row:* scent, pail, breaks *Bottom row:* mane, rain, steel

Page 211 1. quackers 2. fired 3. barking 4. lions 5. syllable 6. diving 7. racket 8. squeak 9. Launch

Page 212 Meanings will vary.

Page 213 *Lines between:* Her eyes were–as big as pizzas. The kangaroo jumped–as high as the stars. The boxes were–as heavy as rocks. The thirsty boy–drank like a fish. The motor–sounds like a hive of bees. The light on the water–looks like diamonds. The ticking clock is–a time bomb. The little puppy is–a real clown. This room is–an oven.; answers will vary

Page 214 Descriptions will vary.

Page 215

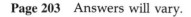

Page 216 *Player 1:* hear, insect, sing, brush, king, clean *Player 2:* fins, time, write, shape, breakfast, country

Page 217 *Top–possible answers:* animals or farm animals, tools *Bottom:* answers will vary

Page 218 Lists will vary.

Page 219 Poems will vary.

Page 220 Words will vary.

Page 221 *Orange:* pierce, brought, pounce, crumb, munch, shrink, hoarse, thread *Yellow:* quarter, order, tiptoe, schoolyard, whether, village, cloudburst, explode *Green:* important, passenger, history, relative *Blue:* society, mechanical, caterpillar, unfortunate, underwater, ingredient, arithmetic, revolution *Red:* unbelievable, congratulations, international, university, opportunity, auditorium, refrigerator, imagination

Page 222 Results will vary.

Page 223 1. car–Cass cat climbed creaky cupboards.–curb 2. pail–Pale Pat picked pineapples proudly.–prove 3. am–Amazing Arthur astonished athletic Ava.–away 4. tear–Ten terrified tigers tiptoed to town.–two 5. when–Whistling wiggling worms worried wrestlers.–wring

Page 224 Answers will vary.

Page 225 *Entry word:* de•li•cious *Pronunciation:* (di lish′əs) *Part of speech:* adjective *Definition:* very pleasing to the senses of taste and smell *Sentence:* The freshly baked bread smelled delicious.
Entry word: rein•deer *Pronunciation:* (rān′dēr′) *Part of speech:* noun *Definition:* a large deer with antlers that lives in cold, northern regions *Sentence:* The reindeer pulled the sleigh across the icy field.

Page 226 Results will vary.

Page 227 1. Lightning Lobby 2. Dead End 3. Spider Den 4. east 5. north 6. Mummy Parlor 7. Evil Entry

Page 228 Results will vary, but most students should find the words are used most often in this order: *the, of, and, to, a, in.*

Page 229 *Crossed-out sentences:* Stephanie's older sister was also an actress. Once Bobby played on a park bench through a rainstorm. Reid also likes to surf and water ski. Her father sold airplanes and there was an airfield behind her house.; young people who have done unusual or interesting things

Page 230 *Robots:* Under some conditions, robot workers are better workers than humans. *Franklin Pierce:* President Pierce wanted to get more land for the United States. *Fruits and Vegetables:* Some people grow giant fruits and vegetables. *Insects:* The life-span of living things varies greatly. *Star:* A star does not last forever. *Brain:* Without your brain, you could not do anything.

Page 231 1. Schoolhouse 2. Mr. and Mrs. Bridges 3. Gold Mine, Jail 4. herb jars, flour sack 5. outlaws 6. Gold Mine 7. Miss Hastings; answers will vary

Page 232 Results and answers will vary.

Page 233 1. *Possible answers:* The object is a large box-shaped container. It stands on legs or rests on a table or shelf. One side of the container has a piece of glass that people look at. The container has controls. The controls make the glass light up in several colors. People watch images parade across the glass. Music and speech come from the container. 2. a television set or watching television 3. Headlines will vary, but should indicate the main idea of the article. 4. Pictures will vary, but should show a modern-day television set.

Page 234 Paragraphs will vary.

Page 235 *Lines between:* Rosa–She jogged more than two miles. Oscar–He had caught a giant fish. Jill–It sailed high into the sky. Agnes–A large group gathered to listen. Ray–He went racing toward the lake. Kenzo–He was sold out in less than an hour.; watermelon

Page 236 Stories will vary.

Page 237 Cooking: *Kids in the Kitchen, How to Make Pizza, Cooking is Fun* Animals: *A Trip to the Zoo, What Swims in the Ocean?, Birdwatcher's Handbook* Sports: *Sports Jokes & Riddles, Play Ball!, Soccer for Everyone* People: *The Little People, The Lost Prince, Telephone Twins;* answers will vary

Page 238 I woke up and looked out my window. The ground was covered with snow. I got washed and took off my pajamas. I put on my warm winter clothes. I ran out into the snow. I built a huge snowhouse. All day long I played in my snowhouse. I got up very early the next day. It was very warm inside. The weather report said it had also gotten warm outside. I ran to look out the window. My snowhouse had melted to the ground!

Page 239 *Fact Set 1:* c *Fact Set 2:* b *Fact Set 3:* c *Fact Set 4:* a *Fact Set 5:* c *Fact Set 6:* b

Page 240 *Place 1:* circus *Place 2:* football game *Place 3:* fire station; results will vary

Page 241 *The Record:* hurricane near Florida *The Gazette:* sudden winter storm *The Sun:* escaped farm animals *The News:* movie star disappeared *The Advance:* scientists using powerful new telescopes; reasons will vary

Page 242 Results will vary.

Page 243 cowboy

Page 244 Names and questions will vary.

Page 245 1. e 2. n. 3. g 4. i 5. n 6. e 7. e 8. r 9. s; engineers

Page 246 Answers and results will vary.

Page 247 Answers will vary.

Page 248 Answers and posters will vary.

Page 249 Ideas and stories will vary.

Page 250 Story maps will vary.

Page 251 1. F 2. F 3. O 4. F 5. F 6. F 7. O 8. O 9. F 10. F 11. O 12. F 13. O 14. F; facts and opinions will vary

Page 252 *Top row:* fact, opinion, fact, fact *Second row:* opinion, fact, opinion, opinion *Third row:* fact, opinion, opinion, fact *Bottom row:* fact, fact, fact, opinion

Page 253 *Crisp O's:* Words That Work, Inc. *Song Saver Super System:* Sell Well Productions, *Snip and Clip:* Creative Copy Company *Hopping Hitops:* Ads Unlimited

Page 254 Notes, ads, and pictures will vary.

Page 255 1. arctic 2. volcano 3. skeleton 4. moon 5. fossil 6. weather 7. fog 8. radio 9. satellite 10. eye 11. insect; Albert Einstein

s	a	t	e	l	l	i	t	e
k	v	o	l	c	a	n	o	f
e	a	r	l	b	r	s	e	o
l	m	r	a	t	c	e	f	s
e	e	o	i	d	t	c	o	s
t	y	n	o	s	i	t	g	i
o	t	e	e	n	c	o	i	l
n	n	w	e	a	t	h	e	r

Page 256 *Augustus Caesar:* Rome *George Washington:* USA *Mahatma Gandhi:* India *Confucius:* China *William II:* Germany *Pericles:* Greece

Page 257 Answers, stories, and drawings will vary.

Page 258 Time lines and stories will vary.

Page 259 Answers may vary.

Page 260 Stories will vary.

Page 261 Shape poems will vary.

Page 262 Poems will vary.

Page 263 *Possible answers:* 1. He learned not to be greedy. 2. You probably are successful in all you do and make a lot of money from your activities. 3. answers will vary

Page 264 Results will vary.